W9-ADZ-432

Visuals Matter!

Designing and Using Effective Visual Representations to Support Project and Portfolio Decisions

Joana Geraldi

Dipl.-Wirt-Ing., Dr-Ing., APMP
Associate Professor
Engineering Systems Group
DTU Management Engineering, Lyngby, DK
Honorary Senior Research Associate
Bartlett, School of Construction and Project Management
University College London, London, UK

Mario Arlt

DPM, M.S., PMP
Group Vice President, Project Management
ABB, Inc., Princeton, NJ, USA

Library of Congress Cataloging-in-Publication Data

Geraldi, Joana G., 1979- author.
   Visuals matter! : designing and using effective visual representations to support project and portfolio decisions / Joana Geraldi.
      pages cm
   Includes bibliographical references.
   ISBN 978-1-62825-078-7 (pbk. : alk. paper) -- ISBN 1-62825-078-X (pbk. : alk. paper)
1. Visual communication. 2. Project management. 3. Communication in management.
I. Title.
   P93.5.G457 2015
   658.4'52--dc23

                                                                    2015028274

ISBN: 978-1-62825-078-7

Published by: Project Management Institute, Inc.
                 14 Campus Boulevard
                 Newtown Square, Pennsylvania 19073-3299 USA
                 Phone: +610-356-4600
                 Fax: +610-356-4647
                 Email: customercare@pmi.org
                 Internet: www.PMI.org

©2015 Project Management Institute, Inc. All rights reserved.

"PMI", the PMI logo, "PMP", the PMP logo, "PMBOK", "PgMP", "Project Management Journal", "PM Network", and the PMI Today logo are registered marks of Project Management Institute, Inc. The Quarter Globe Design is a trademark of the Project Management Institute, Inc. For a comprehensive list of PMI marks, contact the PMI Legal Department.

PMI Publications welcomes corrections and comments on its books. Please feel free to send comments on typographical, formatting, or other errors. Simply make a copy of the relevant page of the book, mark the error, and send it to: Book Editor, PMI Publications, 14 Campus Boulevard, Newtown Square, PA 19073-3299 USA.

To inquire about discounts for resale or educational purposes, please contact the PMI Book Service Center.

         PMI Book Service Center
         P.O. Box 932683, Atlanta, GA 31193-2683 USA
         Phone: 1-866-276-4764 (within the U.S. or Canada) or +1-770-280-4129 (globally)
         Fax: +1-770-280-4113
         Email: info@bookorders.pmi.org

Printed in the United States of America. No part of this work may be reproduced or transmitted in any form or by any means, electronic, manual, photocopying, recording, or by any information storage and retrieval system, without prior written permission of the publisher.

The paper used in this book complies with the Permanent Paper Standard issued by the National Information Standards Organization (Z39.48—1984).

10 9 8 7 6 5 4 3 2 1

Table of Contents

Acknowledgments

Despite their importance, it seems that we still know relatively little about how visuals work. How do visuals influence our thinking, communication, and action in the project and portfolio management context? The question intrigued and fascinated us and inspired our research.

It was back in 2010 at the PMI® Research and Education Conference in Washington, DC, that we met and discovered our joint interest in visualization in the project management context and planted the seeds for this research project. Four years later, we look back at countless discussions, reflections, and two years of intensive research, study, and work. The result of this process is summarized in this book.

This research would not have been possible without the support of several people and institutions. First, we would like to thank the Project Management Institute and the Bartlett School of Construction and Project Management, University College London for providing funding and support throughout the research project. In particular, we would like to express our dear gratitude to Dr. Carla Messikomer and Dr. Harvey Maylor for accompanying us throughout the project, making insightful and relevant recommendations, and acting flexibly to the changing demands during the project. We would like to extend our appreciation to Professor Dr. Peter W. G. Morris and Dr. Andrew Edkins for their critical support as scholars and department heads of the Bartlett School of Construction and Project Management during the project, and for their enlightening suggestions and comments since the research proposal stage.

Our thanks also go to Professor Dr. Katrin Moeslein and Professor Dr. Hagen Habicht from the Peter Pribilla Foundation for the permission and encouragement to reuse and expand on research ideas and findings of the "Solve Different" research project. We would like to extend our gratitude to Professor Bernhard Rothbucher and Professor Oliver Fritz for the insightful dialogue and literature recommendations in the area of data visualization and design. These impulses inspired our thinking and reflections in this area.

We are particularly thankful to Aleksandra Kozawska and Anna Urbaniak, who played a central role in the design of the visuals and the management of the experiment, respectively. Their exceptional professionalism, expert knowledge, and readiness to help were fundamental to this research project.

The planning and execution of the experiment counted on the work of many people. In this respect, we extend our warmest gratitude to Rashed Khandker and Serge Egelman for the programming support, John Kevin and Michael Logie for providing us with the facilities for the experiment, and Elaine Axby and Saule Sakenova for their support during the experiment with management students. Special thanks also go to all those people who participated in the survey and experiment. This research would not have been possible without their collaboration.

Administration support was fundamental to cope with our geographically spread research team (in the United Kingdom, the United States, Germany, Denmark, and Italy). In this respect, we would like to express our gratitude to Sue Anderson for accounting support and Peter Ronan and George Burridge for their help in a wide range of activities.

Last but not least, we would like to thank our families; this research effort would not have been possible without their tremendous support.

Joana Geraldi
Mario Arlt
Princeton and Copenhagen, May 2015

Executive Summary

The Research Problem and Question

This book is the result of a two-year research project, funded by the Project Management Institute (PMI) and University College London (UCL), to explore how visuals can be used and designed in the project, program, and portfolio contexts, and with what effects. Visuals are integral to how we manage projects; consider, for example, Gantt charts, stakeholder maps, traffic lights. Visuals are an opportunity to think sharper, quicker, and clearer. Yet, they also constitute a threat, can bias decisions, and can encourage detrimental behaviors. Project managers and researchers alike have paid little attention to visuals and how they can be used mindfully. The intent of this book is to increase the awareness of project practitioners and scholars about the importance of visuals and to provide guidance on how they can be used and designed.

The research underpinning this book is focused on the impact of visuals on cognition and communication in project portfolio decisions. Our empirical research delves further into the role of visuals in cognition. Cognition is critical in this context. The complexity of portfolio problems quickly exceeds human cognitive limitations as a result of a large number of possible combinations of projects in a portfolio, project interdependencies, a high degree of uncertainty (as future outcomes are unknown and goals and constraints change over time), and the need to balance different and changing objectives of multiple stakeholders.

Irrationality in the behavior of decision makers constitutes an additional challenge, an aspect that is widely studied in decision theory and mostly neglected by the current project management literature. When making decisions, executives are both rational and intuitive. Although intuition is important, we contend that the analysis and use of data is pivotal to address the complexity of portfolios and to make effective decisions.

Visuals can help, as they are a powerful cognition aid. Therefore, this research contributes to a better understanding of the use and design of visuals, and how they can support cognition in portfolio decisions.

Specifically, our goal was to better understand what role visuals can play in portfolio decisions, and how the use and design of visuals can influence cognition in portfolio decisions, and ultimately help project and portfolio management practitioners enhance their visual literacy.

Context of the Research

The Challenge: Portfolio Decisions

Project portfolio management (PPM) can be complex; it is a dynamic and political decision process that typically involves a group of decision makers who periodically select, balance, review, and terminate projects. Early approaches to PPM reduced project portfolio decisions to mathematical optimization problems and emulated techniques from financial portfolio management, namely modern portfolio theory. In reality project portfolio decisions are also social processes, characterized by the involvement of multiple actors and affected by the preferences, biases, and political interests of individuals and groups.

Three types of complexity impact PPM: 1) structural complexity, resulting from the large number of potential portfolios due to the possible combinations of projects, and interdependencies between projects; 2) uncertainty, due to the lack of information, the stochastic nature of future outcomes, and changing goals and constraints; and 3) socio-political complexity, resulting from "bounded rationality" of decision makers, group dynamics, as well as varying and changing objectives of individuals involved.

The Opportunity: Conscious Design and Use of Visuals

If properly constructed or selected, visuals can help address the complexity involved in portfolio decisions. Visuals can be powerful cognition aids, as they impact sensemaking, which is the process of creating a frame of reference to give meaning to a situation, which will inform actions and decisions.[1] Visuals can support sensemaking and ultimately decisions by:

- encouraging engagement with different perspectives on the multifaceted portfolio problem, for example, portfolio balance, strategic alignment, maximization of financial value, identification of projects that do not meet threshold, and so on;
- enabling decision makers to more effectively process large amounts of data and solve problems quicker and more accurately;
- improving clarity, since complex relationships can be understood more easily and quickly than through textual information;
- leveraging our natural abilities to rapidly recognize visual patterns; and
- extending the short-term memory, which is otherwise very limited.

Therefore, visuals help cope with structural complexity and uncertainty, reduce cognitive biases, support negotiation and discovery processes, and hence address socio-political complexity.

Yet, despite such benefits, visuals can also influence communication and cognition in a negative and detrimental way. For example, visuals can intensify insignificant differences through inconsistent scales, falsely instill confidence through their professional look, or encourage unwarranted comparisons. Regardless of whether such effects are consciously designed or not, their influence on decisions remains, as visuals have become part of portfolio decisions.

---

[1] Sensemaking is an active, two-way, and iterative process through which people find or construct a story to account for the data in their own frame of reference, based on information available to them, their goals, experience, convictions, commitment, emotions, and so forth. Continuous try-out of new frames and reframing takes place, especially in a group setting: Negotiating and group sensemaking set in.

Many types of visuals are used in project portfolio management, for example, bubble charts, treemaps, heatmaps, Gantt charts, decision trees, and others. Although certain types of visuals recur in the literature and in practice, there is little consciousness about the importance of designing or selecting the best possible visual for a task at hand. Hence, learning more about how visuals impact our thinking is critical to project and portfolio management.

Tapping into the Potential: Enhancing Visual Literacy

Enhancing visual literacy involves the development of three critical abilities: 1) the ability to *design* visuals (i.e., to consciously produce, compose, and create visual messages); 2) the ability to *use* them effectively; and 3) the awareness of the importance of *users' and designers'* idiosyncrasies, such as experience, familiarity, and emotional reactions to visuals. Our literature review conveys insights to help project practitioners develop competencies in these three areas. Most of these insights are condensed in the five guiding principles for visual design and use in the context of portfolio decisions, summarized in the table below:

Table 1   Overview of Guiding Principles for Visual Design

Principle	Explanation
Interactive	Visual allows users to change and organize data and parameters within an established structure.
Purposeful	Visual addresses at least one relevant perspective of a portfolio problem.
Truthful	Visual displays relevant data accurately.
Efficient	Visual takes advantage of our natural ability to interpret. It consciously displays the maximum amount of information in the smallest space possible so the visual can be processed rapidly and accurately.
Aesthetic	Visual is perceived as harmonious, professional, and beautiful.

Our Methodology

The conclusions from our literature review, research, and practitioner experiences were translated into research propositions that were tested through a human subject experiment with 204 UCL students. Participants of the experiment were asked to select a project portfolio for a company and provided a choice set of 16 projects available for consideration, a prescribed strategy statement, a set of defined financial and nonfinancial goals, and portfolio-level funding and resource constraints. Participants made decisions based on four different dashboards, constructed with visuals that exhibited varying degrees of adherence to the five visual design principles. The different dashboards were randomly assigned to participants to support an identical portfolio decision assignment and in some cases to repeat the assignment with a different dashboard. Variables of interest (i.e., demographics and individual differences that could have influenced decisions) were assessed through post-experimental interviews and a survey.

VISUALS MATTER!

Summary of Findings and Practical Relevance

Based on our experimental and literature research, a set of practical recommendations for designing and using visuals both in general and in PPM-specific contexts has been established:

Recommendation 1: Design visuals carefully. Purposeful visuals enhance cognition and help improve decision quality and lead to more consistent results across different decision makers. Interactive visuals can further increase sensemaking and portfolio decisions.

Recommendation 2: Use visuals consciously. Visuals should support insight from multiple relevant perspectives that are inherent in the decision problem. Although too many—especially unfamiliar—visuals may overwhelm the decision maker, an insufficient use of visuals will limit the understanding and the ability to "see" different perspectives. Purposeful use of visuals takes into consideration 1) how, why, and when to use a particular type of visual; and 2) what combination of visuals to use so as to embrace relevant perspectives of the portfolio decision as effectively as possible. The careful use of new, unfamiliar visuals—provided they are purposeful—will enhance your visual literacy with time. Lastly, a critical engagement with visuals (e.g., identifying filters, omissions, distortions, and presented and missing perspectives) provides insight into what interests a visual may represent.

Recommendation 3: Pay attention to the target audience. Familiar visuals should be used especially for a complex and unfamiliar context in which they can enhance the decision maker's confidence. When given the choice, participants of our experiment preferred familiarity over good design; hence, new visuals, even if well designed, may face some resistance. Guidance may be required to encourage and enable users to effectively engage with visuals. User feedback may help further improve visuals as people have valuable intuitive visuals skills.

Recommendation 4: Be careful about changing and introducing new visuals. Even if visuals are well designed, there is a need to introduce new ones carefully, and to mind the potential learning curve necessary for the visuals to be used effectively. The acceptance of new visuals can be increased if they adhere to the design principles, and are used in combination with well-known visuals. Our results suggest that a change to well-designed visuals is worthwhile, as cognition and decision quality improve. Interestingly, such improvements have not shown a necessary impact on confidence levels: Confidence and decision quality are not strongly related.

In conclusion, it is critical to educate portfolio decision makers, project managers, and project team members on how to use visuals in a mindful way. As common sense would suggest, a map in the hands of two different

people navigating unknown territory may lead to different outcomes.
The same applies to project and portfolio charts. A "visually literate" decision maker who understands both the capabilities and potential limitations of a particular visual will have an enhanced understanding of
the territory and potential navigation routes and his or her decisions will
benefit as a result.

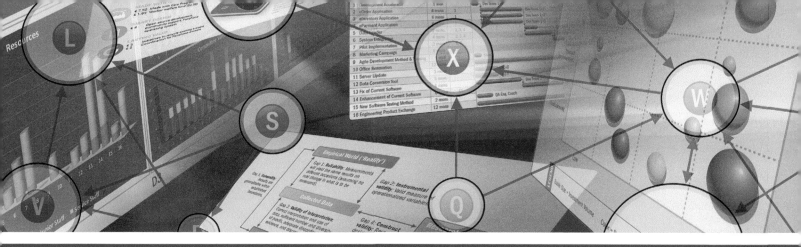

CHAPTER 1

Introduction

Visuals are omnipresent in organizations today. They are artifacts like infographics, tables, maps, diagrams, networks, graphics, but also flip chart drawings, sketches, comics, photos. Nearly all tools in project, program, and portfolio management, and many in management are based on visuals; they are part of how we manage organizations (Meyer, Höllerer, Jancsary, & Van Leeuwen, 2013). If used mindfully, visuals are powerful cognition and communication aids (Card, Mackinlay, & Shneiderman, 1999; Ware, 2012), yet they can also influence our actions and decisions unfavorably.

Scant research has been dedicated to the role of visuals in organizations. In practice, many managers exhibit a low degree of literacy and consciousness in the engagement with visuals (Whyte, Ewenstein, Hales, & Tidd, 2008) and fail to exploit the potential that they have to offer.

The intent of this book is to contribute to addressing these current gaps. The book is the result of a two-year research project, funded by the Project Management Institute (PMI) and University College London (UCL), with the objective to explore how visuals can be used and designed in the project, program, and portfolio contexts, and with what effects. We have focused on the question of how visuals can aid cognition of data in portfolio decisions, and what visuals represent project portfolio data. The objective of this book is twofold: first of all, to increase the awareness of project and portfolio management practitioners and scholars about the importance of visuals, and second, to provide practical recommendations on how visuals can be used and designed in a mindful manner.

1.1 Research Problem and Purpose

The book focuses on the influence of visuals on project portfolio decisions. As researchers and practitioners in the field of project, program, and portfolio management, we selected this specific context because problems and decisions are becoming increasingly complex—a fact that is evident in portfolio decisions. The available information used to support decisions is often vast, ever-changing, ambiguous, and characterized by uncertainties and interdependencies among various decision parameters (Archer & Ghasemzadeh, 1999).

Early literature reduced project portfolio decisions to mathematical optimization problems and emulated techniques from financial portfolio management, namely modern portfolio theory. In reality, project portfolio decisions are social processes, characterized by the involvement of multiple actors and driven by the persuasion of individuals and groups, as well as political interest. Portfolios exhibit a degree of complexity that easily exceeds the human ability to achieve optimal decisions through mere intuition. Portfolios are subject to high uncertainty and change, which further complicates the decision process. Last but not least, the assumption of rationally behaving decision makers only holds to a certain degree. Due to a wide range of observed cognitive mistakes, the behavior of decision makers can be best described as bounded rationality (Simon, 1955) in this context.

Although we are aware that visuals cannot simply dissolve the challenges involved in portfolio decisions, they can help individuals and groups, such as portfolio boards, to overcome them. If used in a mindful manner, they leverage natural perception skills, improve our ability to process information, and thereby help overcome cognitive limitations and provide accelerated and improved insight into decision problems. Furthermore, visuals can be used thoughtfully to help channel the sensemaking process of individuals or groups, to support the negotiation process, and to develop a shared understanding of available data. Finally, even if not used consciously, visuals still impact cognition and communication processes.

It is therefore critical to understand the effect of visuals and how to tap into their potential. That is the aim of this research. Specifically, our empirical analysis explores how the visual display of data can improve portfolio decisions and proposes visualization principles that encourage more informed decisions.

1.2 Research Area and Approach

Understanding the role of visuals in portfolio decisions requires insight into more than one discipline. Therefore, the research that underpins this book took place at the intersection of four areas: 1) project portfolio management, and in particular portfolio decision making[2]; 2) behavioral strategy; 3) organization theory; and 4) data visualization.

---

[2] Decision theory is a rich and complex body of knowledge. It provides the basis for our understanding of portfolio decisions, in particular with regard to data cognition. Yet, our engagement with the current literature on decision theory is cursory. We have opted instead to focus on organization theory and data visualization. Both bodies of literature are currently exploring the role of visuals in decisions (and in organizations), but remain disconnected. This study can therefore act as a bridge between the two areas, and bring some of the insights from data visualization into organization theory.

We study the use of visuals in the context of project portfolio management, and in particular, portfolio decision making. Project portfolio decisions are a classic type of strategic decision-making process. With the spread of projects in organizations, such decisions grow in relevance. Research in the field is needed to build on realistic assumptions about human cognition and behavior (Blichfeldt & Eskerod, 2008; Martinsuo, 2013). In this respect, project portfolio management would profit from a stronger relationship with the reemerging field of behavioral strategy.

Behavioral strategy applies cognitive and social psychology to improve our understanding of how executives formulate strategic decisions (Schranger & Madansky, 2013). "Behavioral strategy aims to bring realistic assumptions about human cognition, emotions, and social behavior to strategic management of organizations and, thereby, to enrich strategy theory, empirical research, and real-world practice" (Powell, Lovallo & Fox, 2011, p. 1371). Building on relevant and rigorous research, the field contributes not only to the theoretical understanding of strategic decisions, but also to the development of pragmatic solutions, that can help executives cope with our cognitive limitations and improve decisions.

Organization theory provides insight into the visual dimension of organizations (e.g., Bell, Warren, & Schroeder, 2014; Meyer et al., 2013; Puyou, Quattrone, Mclean, & Thrift, 2012). The salient literature provided our research effort with a sociological and critical perspective of visuals. It discusses, for example, how visuals are used as a rhetorical device, and how they function differently from verbal language. Although the visual dimension is a broad subject in itself and involves all that is visible in organizations, this book is focused only on visual representation (i.e., on *visuals* instead of on *what is visible*).

The literature on data visualization provides a more technical and pragmatic understanding of visuals. It draws mainly on neuroscience (i.e., how the human brain processes visuals) and also hinges on the knowledge of designers and architects. From the data visualization literature we captured theories and practical recommendations for the design and use of visuals. This area addresses problems related to visual representations and visualization. We define visual representations (or visuals) as artifacts (i.e., graphics, logos, paintings, photography, sketches, and charts) that support the visualization process. Visualization is the cognitive process through which we make sense of the visual world around us and help us in the development of our own mental models (Mazza, 2009). Although we discuss some aspects of visualization, our focus is on visuals.

The four aforementioned areas provide the ingredients for both a pragmatic and a critical understanding of the role of visuals in portfolio decisions. Our theoretical contribution lies in bringing well-known issues identified in cognitive psychology to bear in project portfolio literature, and developing pragmatic solutions to use visuals to improve cognition in decisions. Therefore, our efforts aim to contribute not only to the field of project and portfolio management but also to behavioral strategy. For the interested reader, Appendix A offers a brief historical overview and current trends of data visualization and organization theory perspectives on visuals.

1.3 Research Phases

Our approach consisted of four phases (see Table 1.1).

Table 1.1—Phases of the research.

Phases	Description
Literature and practice review	• Project portfolio management literature • Analysis of visuals in portfolio management • Survey
Concept development	• Visualization and sensemaking • Theoretical development • Propositions
Experimental validation	• Experimental design • Experiment
Analysis	• Quantitative analysis • Qualitative data • Conclusions

Naturally, our exploration of the topic was not entirely sequential and linear: For example, survey results and trial runs of the experiment triggered reflection, influenced concept development, and led to adjustments and refinement of our thinking throughout this research effort.

In a sense, our approach was similarly iterative, like the portfolio selection process: Just like the participants in our experiment, portfolio decision makers typically interact with data and observe outcomes as they simulate various portfolio scenarios until they achieve a feasible and meaningful portfolio mix.

Each of the above phases produced several outputs, which are summarized in this book.

1.4 Target Audience, Structure, and Layout of the Book

This book attempts to appeal to both academic and practitioner audiences. We recognize that straddling both audiences is no easy task: While we are trying to provide a coherent story for academics throughout the book, we recommend Chapters 1, 2, and Section 4.6 to both audiences, as they cover the aforementioned literature and practice review.

Chapter 3 and most of Chapter 4 develop the propositions of this work, and are therefore a dense read. Yet, the chapters should provide insight to anyone who is interested in understanding why visuals are powerful and affect our sensemaking process, and in particular, our thinking, communication, and action. We have attempted to write the chapters in an accessible manner, so that previous knowledge on sensemaking and visual design are not required to fully grasp the concepts.

Practitioners may also choose to skip Chapter 5 (Research Design) and Chapter 6 (Data Analysis) and rejoin the journey in Chapter 7, where findings are summarized, including those from the experimental research.

The book uses numerous visuals throughout to provide examples and illustrations of our story. Last but not least, we want to provide practitioners with inspiration and aids for practical application.

CHAPTER 2

The Challenge: Project Portfolio Decisions

2.1 PPM Context and Its Challenges

As the Project Management Institute predicted in their *Industry Growth Forecast* (PMI, 2013), the importance of project management continues to increase in project-intensive industries globally. As a result, attention to the management of portfolios of projects has been increasing; both in the private and the public sectors, organizations have been attempting to deliver more and larger projects, to achieve higher project success rates and do so under greater complexity and resource constraints. Project portfolio management helps organizations achieve these goals.

Project portfolio management (PPM) is a centralized, dynamic, complex, and political decision process in which portfolios of projects, programs, and other activities are constantly updated and revised, and ongoing projects may be accelerated, terminated, or continued according to plan (Cooper, Edgett, & Kleinschmidt, 2001). Its objective is to act as a bridge or hub between organizational strategy and project execution (Levine, 2005) with the goal to achieve specific strategic objectives through the selection and successful execution of projects, while using scarce resources effectively. Specifically, the literature recognized three goals of project portfolio management (Artto, Martinsuo, & Aalto, 2001; Cooper et al., 2001; Dye & Pennypacker, 1999):

> *Strategic alignment* can be defined as the linkage of portfolios with the long-term objectives of an organization (Artto & Dietrich, 2004; Cooper et al., 2001), whereby project portfolios must be pursued to maximize

the probability of achieving an articulated vision and thereby realizing the organizational strategy.

Portfolio balancing is the second objective of project portfolio management (Cooper et al., 2001), and various qualitative and quantitative approaches have been introduced in the literature (Caron, Fumagalli, & Rigamonti, 2007). Portfolio balancing deals with the recognition and decision of trade-offs in the pursuit of alternative portfolios, for example, risk versus reward, cost to implement versus time to market, and technical feasibility versus market attractiveness (Cooper et al., 2001).

Lastly, *benefits maximization,* or the achievement of the maximum possible utility under given constraints, is the third objective. In a commercial context, financial performance indicators (e.g., ROI [Return on Investment], and NPV [net present value]) or risk-adjusted metrics are typically used, as well as composite metrics, such as scorecards that allow inclusion of nonfinancial benefits metrics (Norrie, 2006).

Project portfolio management and its related decisions cannot be reduced to a rational decision and optimization problem due to the inherent complexity of portfolio decision making. In order to better understand the complexity challenge in portfolio decisions, we draw on previous work on complexity in decision making (Snowden & Boone, 2007), in strategy (Stacey, 1995), in project management (Geraldi, Maylor, & Williams, 2011; Maylor, Turner, & Murray-Webster, 2013), and in portfolio management (Arlt, 2010). We discern three types of complexity, which are explored in the next sections.

2.2 Structural Complexity

Structural complexity involves the ability of decision makers to evaluate a high number of combinations in light of complex interdependencies among projects and multiple and contradicting goals.

The number of possible combinations of projects in a portfolio grows exponentially with the number of candidate projects. Even for a relatively small portfolio of 16 projects, 65,536 combinations of portfolio choice sets are theoretically possible.

Yet, not all of the aforementioned theoretically possible combinations are feasible, because constraints impact the actual choice set. First, decision makers aim to achieve multiple, sometimes conflicting, goals (Archer & Ghasemzadeh, 1996), and attend to restricting and complicated resources constraints (e.g., the number of staff with a certain skill set, and their availability over time).

Second, projects rarely exist in isolation and portfolio decisions need to consider their different interdependencies. The classic understanding of project interdependencies draws on project management's task interdependencies, and explores schedule-driven interdependencies (e.g., Project 2 can only be started after Project 1 has been completed) (Levine, 2005). Schmidt (1993) looks at the interdependency problem from a portfolio perspective and proposes benefit, outcome, and resource "interactions" between projects. The interesting insight from Schmidt is to realize that at the portfolio level, interdependencies are not merely related to the completion of tasks, but can also depend on the realization of benefits or the creation of a certain outcome. Verma and Sinha (2002) further specify the kinds of interactions that exist between projects and analyze resource and technology interdependencies. Arlt (2010) integrates and enhances both perspectives, and suggests five types of interdependencies. We draw on Arlt and propose six interdependencies:

- Benefit (utility) interdependencies: These refer to 1) Schmidt's notion of benefit interdependency, and 2) the potential to gain benefits greater than the sum of a single project's benefits.
- Risk interdependencies: These refer to whether risks of different projects can be compensated or amplified by one another.
- Financial interdependencies: The execution of a project can result in financial gains or losses by other projects.
- Outcome interdependencies: The achievement of a desired outcome of a project is required in order to achieve the outcome of another.
- Schedule interdependencies: Similar to the task interdependencies between projects, these refer to how projects are interrelated in terms of time; for example, it would be advantageous to conduct Project 1 and Project 2 simultaneously.
- Resources: This refers to the dependency of different projects in the portfolio on the same resources.

The identification of interdependencies does not suffice to manage them. It is also important to recognize that such dependencies can be more or less strong in different portfolios (Arlt, 2010).

Lastly, the variety of project types also increases the structural complexity of project portfolios. Each different type of project has specific characteristics and requires different types of governance and sponsorship, leading to different and possibly incompatible cultures and conflicting processes and management styles. A portfolio decision body may govern research, development, maintenance, and organizational change projects, all of which exhibit very different characteristics. If the system doesn't accommodate the different projects, organizational actors may opt to leave projects outside of the portfolio management system, so they can be managed differently. However, the downside is that doing so reduces the effectiveness of the portfolio management system as a whole, as reported by Blichfeldt and Eskerod (2008).

From the description of structural complexity, it becomes apparent that selecting the optimal portfolio is a task that quickly exceeds the cognitive abilities of decision makers. In this regard, the use of visual aids can be particularly helpful to make structurally complex portfolio problems more accessible. Visuals, such as network diagrams, are helpful in understanding independencies among projects. Visuals can also help us grasp and compare the different potential combinations of project portfolio and their impact on portfolio benefits.

2.3 Emergent Complexity

Portfolio management and decisions face what Maylor et al. (2013) term *emergent complexity*. This is characterized by potential and actual change in the portfolio. Key decision variables are stochastic rather than deterministic, such as project scope, outcomes, required resources, and delivery dates, and are likely to change over time. Likewise, stakeholders and their power and interests may change. Even the original business case for projects may change or no longer exist at a later point in time. Hence, today's "optimal" portfolio could be less than optimal tomorrow.

Recent research on the topic of uncertainty makes an important distinction between expected and unexpected events. Expected events constitute the materialization of risks and opportunities. Although often perceived as a surprise (Geraldi, Lee-Kelley, & Kutsch, 2010), expected events (or "known unknowns") can be managed through classic risk management. Unexpected events ("unknown unknowns") (Loch, DeMeyer, & Pich, 2006), on the other hand, are a different kind of challenge and demand organizational resilience and mindfulness (Weick & Sutcliffe, 2001).

Uncertainty and changes combined with structural complexity lead to even higher uncertainty (Duncan, 1972). This is because projects are interrelated, and therefore changes in one project will impact others. As portfolios become increasingly structurally complex, they become more interdependent, and interdependent in different ways. This makes it hard to understand how changes in one project will impact the entire portfolio and its ramifications (Perrow, 1999).

Portfolio decisions are even more challenging, because they face epistemic uncertainty—lack of information, lack of agreement over current and future situations, or ambiguity. This increases pressure on decision makers, as they take responsibility and are made accountable for educated guesses.

Hence, there is a need for constant update, revision, and action on the project portfolio (Cooper et al., 2001), including risk management action to respond to uncertainty. These decisions require sensing (i.e., the capture of eminent changes), seizing (to identify necessary organizational responses), and learning through transforming existing and developing new capabilities (Petit & Hobbs, 2010).

Visuals can play an important role in making visible the uncertainties in available data. We often confuse estimates and—at least subconsciously—treat them as de facto and deterministic data, rather than truly as stochastic. Emergent complexity also helps us understand different portfolio scenarios in light of certain events; suitable visuals in this context include decision trees, which are widely used for scenario planning.

Visuals can also call our attention to early signals of change, by, for instance, helping us look at data from different perspectives and identify patterns or unusual relationships among indicators. Finally, visuals can help grasp ambiguity by encouraging comparisons, and can identify "blind spots"—aspects of data that appear to be missing.

2.4 Socio-Political Complexity

Furthermore, portfolio decisions are multidisciplinary in nature and often demand the integration of people from different functional disciplines and cultural backgrounds. Multiple decision makers with different and conflicting objectives further increase complexity. According to Stacey (1995), stakeholders are often far from agreement, which makes the portfolio problem even more complex. Hence, negotiation and persuasion practices are intrinsic to portfolio decisions; stakeholders make sense of a portfolio problem collectively and elaborate in an ongoing, nonlinear, and not completely structured way, converging toward a decision rather than following a strict linear and step-by-step process.[3]

As a consequence, project portfolio decisions do not constitute a straightforward optimization problem that always has a clear best solution. What is "best" depends on the perspective of the stakeholders, which is a result of individual and group interests, but is also based on their belief systems. Even if all stakeholders would be completely altruistic and fully focused on maximizing the benefit to their organization, they would still have divergent opinions about what would be the best solution or even what constitutes benefit.

Visuals are also paramount when acting in complex socio-political contexts. In this regard, visuals are particularly useful as a rhetorical device for persuasion. Visuals are enchantingly, and dangerously, convincing, and can yield legitimacy, professionalism, and exactness, which may not correspond to the nature of the data presented. They also help focus attention on certain aspects of portfolio over others, and hence channel conversations and decisions accordingly. Furthermore, visuals can act as boundary objects, and facilitate the dialogue between different disciplines, cultures, and belief systems (Justesen & Mouritsen, 2009).

Socio-political complexity is also characterized by an individual's cognitive ability. Psychologists have already recognized the cognitive challenges to manage complex systems, namely the limited human capacity to anticipate side effects and unintended consequences of actions (Doerner, 1989), leading to cognitive limitations (Foreman & Selly, 2002; McCray et al., 2002).

"Bounded rationality" (Simon, 1955) and underlying cognitive errors take into account the aspect of human *irrationality* in real-world decision making. Examples of cognitive biases that influence portfolio decisions include optimism bias, overconfidence, recency, illusion of control, group thinking, and conservatism (Shore, 2008). In addition, cognitive errors, such as the ignoring of factors, mistaken hypotheses, or inappropriate comparisons (McCray, Purvis, & McCray, 2002), further reduce the probability of decision success.

---

[3] Portfolio decisions can also follow a "garbage can" model, where, for instance, portfolio board meetings become opportunities for choice, and attract several unrelated and simultaneously available problems and solutions. When acting as "garbage cans," portfolio solutions do not derive from problems; instead, problems and solutions coexist and are matched in a complex and nonlinear process. The decision outcome will depend on the allocation of time and energy to potential choices. In this respect, visuals can help tunnel the attention of stakeholders to certain perspectives of a problem (Cohen, March, & Olsen, 1972).

Behavioral science is evolving and continuing to explore patterns of irrationality. For example, Ariely (2008) observed in his experiments the effects of anchoring (the use of reference data for evaluating or estimating an unknown value) and the role of people's emotional states in decision making, among others. If such aspects of irrationalities are properly understood, their impact can be predicted, or bias in the actual decision can be reduced as a result of awareness of cognitive error.

Hence, a challenge involved in portfolio decisions is irrationality in the behavior of the decision maker (Bazerman, 2009), an aspect that is widely studied in decision-making literature (Eisenhardt & Zbaracki, 1992) and mostly overlooked by current project management literature (Eskerod, Blichfeldt, & Toft, 2004). It is broadly recognized that executives are both rational and intuitive when making decisions (Fredrickson, 1985). Although intuition is critical (Dane & Pratt, 2007; Sadler-Smith & Shefy, 2004), we contend that the rational analysis and use of data is pivotal to address the complexity of portfolios and make effective decisions (Ariely, 2008; Bazerman, 2009; Bourgeois & Eisenhardt, 1988; Omodei, Elliott, Clancy, Wearing, & McLennan, 2005; Staw, 1981; Tversky & Kahneman, 1974).

In this respect, visuals can help us make sense of data, providing a diversity of frames to see the different facets of the portfolio problem, and hence reduce the likelihood of cognitive errors, and thereby ameliorate socio-political complexity.

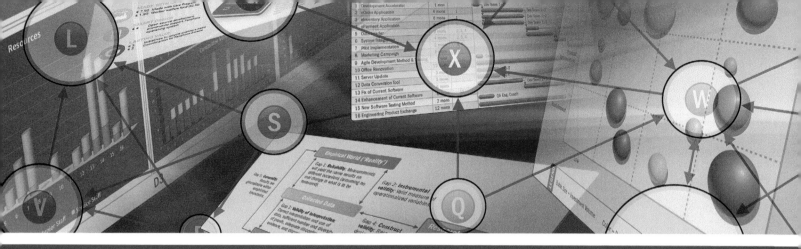

CHAPTER 3

The Opportunity: Visuals

The aim of this chapter is to explore *why* visuals matter in portfolio decisions. The chapter is divided into four parts. The first part delves into the portfolio decision process as a sensemaking process. The second part discusses why visuals are powerful sensemaking aids. It starts with a definition of the term *visual* and its key features, then explores why these features can aid the sensemaking process, in particular communication and cognition, and discusses how visuals can address portfolio decision complexity. The third part points out challenges related to visuals. In the fourth and last part, we introduce the concept of visual literacy and its importance, and refine the goals of the study.

3.1 Portfolio Decision as a Sensemaking Process

Decision making has been an important topic for academics and practitioners alike for at least a century. There are plenty of studies and theories about how decisions are made in general, and in organizations in particular. One of the most recent insights into decision making results from the concept of sensemaking. Sensemaking is used as the frame of reference for portfolio decisions in this study. Our research draws on Klein's data-frame sensemaking model (Klein, Moon, & Hoffman, 2006a, 2006b). We augmented this model with some of Weick's ideas on the topic (Weick, 1995; Weick, Sutcliffe, & Obstfeld, 2005).[4]

---

[4] Sensemaking in organizations and sociology has been heavily influenced by Weick's work. His seminal work is complex, yet insightful, and highly recommended. Yet, we have chosen to draw on Klein et al.'s (2006a, b) model because it is focused on the role of data (experiences, clues, information) in the sensemaking process, and on the individual sensemaking process, instead of Weick's organizational sensemaking. This concept is appropriate to our research, as visuals function as a type of "data" and our empirical focus is on individual cognition, as we explain in Section 3.4.

In simple terms, sensemaking is a process of creating a frame of reference (also known as a mental model). A frame gives meaning to a problem, and thereby guides decisions and actions. Everyone uses frames of reference that help explain the world around us. We are also constantly refining our frames as we interact with our context and sense what scholars term *cues*. Cues include a wide range of things, such as charts and data in project reports, a conversation with stakeholders, or even a strange gesture or look.

We are confronted with cues that may or may not fit our current frames. Sensemaking comes about when there is a misfit between our understanding (frame or frames) and the cues we sensed in our context (Weick, 1995). This misfit can, for example, be a problem, for which one does not have a clear opinion or explanation (Klein, Phillips, Raill, & Peluso, 2007).

As people encounter cues that are inconsistent with their current frames, they can discard the cues and keep an existing the frame, or they can question the frame. The sensemaking process is triggered as current frames are questioned. Therefore, sensemaking is an active process, in which people consciously search for explanations to problems.

For example, a promising project in a portfolio is not delivering the expected outcomes. The current frame, "promising project," doesn't fit the contextual data of poor outcomes. We can now either choose to ignore this mismatch, or try to understand it. This process of understanding (or creating frames) is the sensemaking process.

The process of developing a frame is also a recursive process of fitting cues into frames and the frames into the cues. In this regard, just like Dutch graphic artist M. C. Escher's *Drawing Hands* lithograph, we cannot say which comes first, frames or cues. Yet, to simplify, sensemaking can be reduced to the following process: First, an initial frame is elaborated as one searches and filters data from the context. We then start the process of reframing, in which the first frame (also termed the *anchoring frame*) is questioned, and new, more elaborate frames are constructed. The process is schematically explained in Figure 3.1.

In the process of reframing, we put the emerging frame into question. We search for inconsistencies and anomalies, judge plausibility, and gauge data quality. In the portfolio decision context, decision makers could, for example, ask the following questions: Are all strategic objectives being addressed? Do all selected projects contribute to the strategy? Does the proportion of investment in different strategic objectives correspond to organizational priorities? Do we have a balanced exposure to risk? Are we innovative enough? Do projects address key stakeholders' interests? Does the portfolio maximize benefits? Whose interests does it serve? Does it adhere to (or violate) resource constraints? By asking such questions, different potential frames are compared, combined, and discarded in search of acceptable, coherent new frames. Hence, sensemaking is considered an ongoing process, as data are constantly changing and so are our frames. It is also retrospective, as people search for an understanding of the problem by looking back into what happened and why.

As Klein et al. (2007) explain, "People react to data elements" (or cues) "by trying to find or construct a story, script, a map, or some other type of

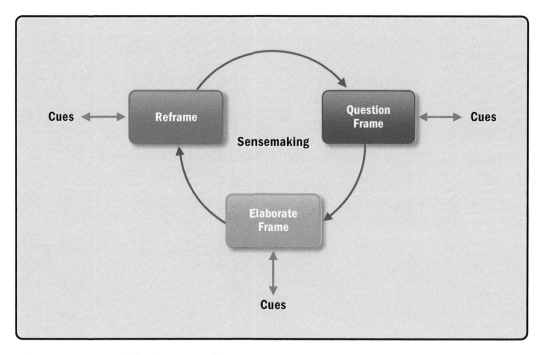

Figure 3.1—Simplified sensemaking process.

structure to account for the data. At the same time, their repertoire of frames—explanatory structures—affects which data elements they consider and how they will interpret these data" (p. 120). That is why sensemaking is considered a two-way process of fitting cues into frame and frame into cues.

In this process, "[t]he specific frame a person uses depends on the data or information that are available and also on the person's goals, the repertoire of the person's frames, and the person's stance (e.g., current workload, fatigue level, and commitment to an activity)" (Klein et al., 2007, p. 134). Therefore, frames are also influenced by personal preferences, experience, specialist knowledge, and political stance, and hence, are idiosyncratic. They also embed a system of rules, principles, and so forth, used in organizing and guiding individual behavior (Goffman, 1974).

Coming back to the example above, organizational actors (executives, project managers, team members, and others) will search for alternative frames to explain why the promising project is underperforming. Each of the actors will try out different frames, according to his or her own experiences, knowledge, and political interests. In this respect, the sensemaking process in organizations is an individual but also a social exercise. The different actors will negotiate meaning (different frames) and can eventually converge into an explanation. For example, the project was not resourced adequately, or there has been a change in the environmental conditions. Obviously, the explanation can be, and usually is, more elaborate than the single factors above exemplified. This explanation will guide decisions and actions (i.e., what to do next).

As the new frame leads to actions, it also shapes the context and changes the situation. That is why the sensemaking process not only responds but also constructs the context around us (Weick et al., 2005). Likewise, it will also inform the development of our identities and roles (Weick, 1995).

Finally, although people seek to develop a coherent frame to understand a specific situation, in complex contexts, it is possible to entertain several, even contradicting frames at a point in time. This in itself is a source of emotional stress in complex situations (Weick, 1995) and one potentially faced in portfolio contexts.

In summary, in this research, sensemaking is understood as a conscious, active, social, idiosyncratic, retrospective, and ongoing process of creating a frame to a disrupting situation or problem. It is based on a two-way process of fitting the cues into a frame and the frame into the cues. In the portfolio context, organizational actors will develop multiple frames, negotiate which of them will become the most accepted, and converge into an understanding that will guide decisions and actions and construct identities. Hence, sensemaking in a portfolio decision context involves both cognition and communication challenges.

Visuals are helpful in this process because they provide the opportunity for alternative perspectives to be expressed. They help people involved in portfolio decisions to "see" and consider these perspectives in the sensemaking process. The next sections delve into the influence of visuals in the sensemaking process.

3.2 The Power of Visuals

This section explains why visuals are particularly powerful artifacts in the sensemaking process. The key to answering this question lies in a deeper understanding of the characteristics of visuals and what makes them different from verbal language (see Section 3.2.1). We further use the characteristics of visuals and the understanding of sensemaking to argue that visuals are critical aids in the sensemaking process, and that they specifically support cognition (Section 3.2.2) and communication (Section 3.2.3). We conclude by summarizing the strengths of visuals in the project portfolio decision context and highlighting how visuals address portfolio complexity (Section 3.2.4).

3.2.1 What Constitutes a Visual

We understand a visual as a physical representation of a referent (i.e., the object represented by the visual) (Pauwels, 2006). This referent can be data, concepts, ideas, objects, people, or projects that are presented in a two-dimensional plane. The next paragraphs describe each element of this definition, the key features of visuals, and how they contribute to sensemaking.

Dimensions of a Plane

Although visuals may represent three or more dimensions, they do so in a two-dimensional device, the plane (Bertin, 1967/2010), which can be, for example, a piece of paper, a wall, or a computer screen.[5] Visuals use the plane in

---

[5] Holographic images or other 3-D technologies stay in the interface between a visual and an object. We are currently less interested in such visuals, as they are not yet relevant in project portfolio contexts.

a very different way than verbal language does. Verbal language draws on our understanding of sound and time; for example, written language uses letters to represent the sounds and punctuation to represent time. Visuals, in contrast, can make use of at least three sensory variables:[6] variations of marks (e.g., different colors and shapes) and the two dimensions of the plane (Bertin, 1967/2010). Visuals can transmit the relationship of three dimensions instantaneously, while verbal language unfolds meaning sequentially and linearly. Time is not a dimension of conventional visual representations; however, dynamic properties are increasingly used. Animations, for example, can display changes in data over time.[7] Such dynamic properties are actually useful in the project and portfolio contexts, yet this does not change the fact that visuals do not require time to transmit information. Thus, nonlinearity and immediacy are key features of visuals. Nonlinearity makes visuals an outstanding display of complex information. Immediacy acts as a holding ground and helps us cope with our short-term memory.

The Translation Process: From Referent to Representation

The design of visuals invariably involves a translation from the referent to a physical representation. A network plan translates tasks and interdependencies (the referent) into a visual, a photo of a person represents the looks of a person (the referent) into a visual, and so on. Concrete objects are usually translated from 3-D format to 2-D format and often scaled down. For example, the geographical map of a country (the visual) is a scaled-down and flattened representation of the country's geographical terrain and a selection of its properties (the referent). Project portfolio visuals can also represent abstract referents, such as schedule, financial, and other data. Visuals of abstract referents are constructed by allocating physical properties to abstract data. For example, the abstract concept of a portfolio budget can be physically represented by the size of the circles in a bubble chart.

Much of the power of visuals lies exactly in *how* this translation is performed. We can be easily tempted to think that a visual is a true depiction of its referent. The blurred line between perception and reality makes visuals enchantingly persuasive, as they display abstract data in a rather objective, concrete, and precise way, regardless of whether the data are precise. As stated by Meyer et al. (2013), visuals transport "specific (normative) ideas behind a veil of seemingly objective representation" (p. 494). This contradiction is at the heart of many of the "tricks" visuals play on us, or we play with them when constructing a visual rhetoric.

Hence, it is critical to remind ourselves that this translation is a choice, and hence, is not neutral. Even photos can be deceptive. The use of different lenses

---

[6] Current technology allows us to develop far more sophisticated visuals that appeal to more sensory variables, such as display 3-D graphics and interactive visuals, where a user actively shapes the visual. In this process, the visuals become an even more powerful cognitive aid.

[7] See, for example, Rosling, who explains the development of health and income in the past 200 years, published on the Gapminder website (http://www.gapminder.org/).

and lighting can easily distort reality. The photographer also decides what is framed in the photo and what is left out; the photo represents, therefore, at best a piece of reality, but not "the reality." The same statement is valid for representations of abstract data (Burri, 2012). Visuals are representations; they are "never innocent or neutral reflections of reality. As the word itself suggests, they re-present reality for us: that is, they offer not a mirror of the world but an interpretation of it" (Midalia, 1999, p. 28, as quoted by Hurrell, 2000). Hence, as we see visuals, we see through the eyes of other people.

What makes visuals even more powerful is their ability to connect with our emotions. This is especially the case when the translation uses vivid images (i.e., visuals that closely resemble reality, like the print ad in Figure 3.2).

Figure 3.2—Award-winning campaign to raise awareness of the risks of secondhand smoke, developed by the Cancer Patients Aid Association (CPAA), India.

Understanding this translation process is therefore critical for a literate design and use (interpretation) of visuals. For example, a photo of a building represents something that exists today. Yet, a 3-D-rendered visual of a future building represents a projection of the future; the building doesn't exist yet and the rendered image gives us a rather realistic, near-photographic image of what it will look like when built. By using such images, architects convey a sense of the legitimacy of the new building (Justesen & Mouritsen, 2009). A sketch, in contrast, provides the exact opposite image, of something that is still a work in progress.[8]

---

[8] We will further explore the translation process and its implications throughout the next chapters, in particular when we discuss the truthful principle in Section 4.6.3.

Cognition entails mental abilities and processes related to knowledge acquisition and development. This includes problem solving, decision making, memory, and learning (Newell, 1990). Cognition can be confused with rational thinking; yet cognition and decisions embrace both rationality and intuition (Eisenhardt & Zbaracki, 1992; Fredrickson, 1985; Newell, 1990).

Cognition mostly takes place by interacting with aids. Visuals constitute powerful tools to enhance cognition (Ware, 2012). They have the potential to improve our ability to see and consider different perspectives of problems. They enhance the ability of a decision maker to process large amounts of data (Smelcer & Carmel, 1997; Ware, 2012), provide insights (Tufte, 2001), and solve problems (Larkin & Simon, 1995) quickly and more accurately (Jarvenpaa, 1989; Jarvenpaa & Dickson, 1988). This is because visuals are particularly good at displaying complex relationships, allowing rapid pattern recognition and acting as an extension of our short-term memory.

Different Perspectives

Visuals are used and useful in cognition because they offer and help us see different perspectives of the portfolio problem. Like a complex geometric form, the portfolio problem has different facets and can be examined through different perspectives. Each visual could provide one or several perspectives of the portfolio problem, for example, an insight into the portfolio balance, the strategic alignment of the projects with the portfolio, or their individual and cumulative benefits contribution. As decision makers analyze different visuals, they engage with different perspectives, which enable them to elaborate, question, and build more comprehensive frames to understand the portfolio problem.

Research shows that decisions are less effective when decision makers rush to portfolio solutions or, conversely, take too much time to decide on an interpretation (Rudolph, 2003). Effective decision makers will quickly commit to a first frame and use it to generate a hypothesis, then conduct effective tests and gradually construct ever more comprehensive frames. Only a limited set of causal factors are used to develop this first interpretation (Klein et al., 2006b). Thus, a purposeful visual can work as such an anchor, because it addresses at least one facet of the portfolio decision problem.

Visuals can also support the next steps in the sensemaking process, as they can trigger questions and instigate reframing. Ideally, perspectives should embrace typical angles or facets of the portfolio decision problem, such as strategic alignment, risk exposure, or project interdependencies. By showing such perspectives, visuals will encourage people to consider these perspectives and help them avoid typical mistakes in portfolio decisions.

Complex Relationships

It is widely recognized that visual representations aid comprehension of complex phenomena and large volumes of data, overcoming cognitive limitations. Unlike text, visuals do not superimpose a linear flow of arguments; visuals are nonlinear.

Therefore, visuals lend themselves to explore more complex relationships between entities, be they tasks, arguments, people, or any other variables of interest. For example, whereas a text is appropriate for the development of arguments in depth with higher degrees of ambiguity and nuances, a visual (i.e., a mindmap) can provide a rich overview of arguments and their relationships more effectively. In this respect, Fichhoff (2006) suggests that creating a visual representation of thought, such as an influence diagram, can improve clarity of thought and reveal vague assumptions, incomplete analyses, and missing information, and therefore improve problem solving.

A seminal example of a visual showing the complex relationships is Charles Minard's map of Napoleon's march to Moscow in 1812 (see Figure 3.3). The map was popularized by Tufte (2001), and impressively conveys the tragic story of Napoleon's march to Moscow through a rich visual. The visual conveys numerous variables, such as temperature, timeline, size of the Napoleonic army, and the army's exact location (latitude and longitude), as well as its direction of movement in a neatly organized plot.

However, the visual was also criticized for being too complex, and so its message does not spring to mind as one gazes at it (Few, 2006). In our opinion, not all visuals need to be understood in the blink of eye. In this case, the visual is telling a story, not advising of an imminent or dangerous situation. It is also part of visual literacy to be able to engage and understand more complex visuals, as well as to produce them purposefully (i.e., recognizing different needs in, for example, the speed of pattern recognition). We will discuss this in more detail in Section 4.6, Guiding Principles for Visual Design.

Several empirical studies confirmed the advantages of visuals over text. For example, Larkin and Simon (1995) compared the effectiveness of diagrams with equivalent text descriptions in solving physics problems. Diagrams were most effective because they reduce the need for labeling and descriptions;

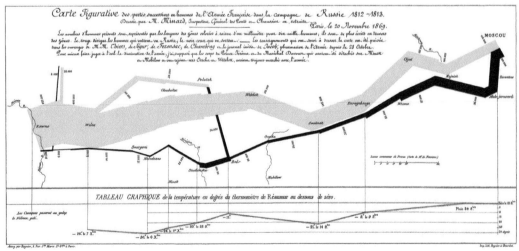

Charles Minard's 1869 chart showing the number of men in Napoleon's 1812 Russian campaign army, their movements, as well as the temperature they encountered on the return path. Lithograph, 62 x 30 cm, retrieved from http://en.wikipedia.org/wiki/File:Minard.png#metadata

Figure 3.3—Example of a visual display of complex information.

because data are organized around two or more dimensions, the reader can establish relationships between variables more easily and quickly. MacNeice (1951) confronted 300 management students with a complex production planning task. When asked to solve it intuitively, only 1% managed to do so successfully. When given a Gantt chart, all students developed a solution within 15 minutes. Smelcer and Carmel (1997) compared the effectiveness of maps and tables to solve managerial problems and established that problems are solved faster and with fewer errors with maps than with tables, particularly as problems become more complex.

This feature of visuals is particularly relevant for understanding the structural complexity of portfolios. For example, the interdependencies between projects are more easily visualized in a network plan than in textual descriptions. Similarly, the relationship among decision variables and especially trade-offs in a portfolio can be easily visualized, with the help of a bubble chart, for example.

Rapid Pattern Recognition

Not only can we visually absorb large amounts of information at once, but we do so extremely efficiently. Take a look at the image depicting the cost breakdown of the Fairphone (Figure 3.4).

Without looking at the details and thoroughly understanding what each color represents, we can immediately see that the pink color dominates; hence, product cost makes up most of the total cost. This immediate recognition can be explained as follows: Low-level properties of visuals, such as color,

Figure 3.4—Cost breakdown of Fairphone. Source: Fairphone (2013).

orientation, texture, and movement are captured accurately and very rapidly in the pre-attentive stage, the first stage of seeing, within 200 to 250 milliseconds (Healey, 2012). Even after the pre-attentive stage, sensemaking through vision is particularly fast, as "the eye and the brain form a massive parallel processor that provides the highest bandwidth channel into human cognition centers" (Ware, 2012, p. 2).

However, not everything can be easily seen. We are particularly good at seeing certain patterns as a result of our natural ability to interpret visuals. For example, Figure 3.4 draws on one of them, namely similarity. The immediate pattern recognition is useful to appreciate and manage a portfolio's structural and emergent complexity. We will explore such patterns in detail in our design principles (see Section 4.6.3).

Extension of the Short-term Memory

Our limited short-term memory constrains our ability to cope with complex problems. We can only hold three to nine "chunks" of information (Few, 2006) and process on average four or fewer variables at a time (Halford, Baker, McCredden, & Bain, 2005). Hence, excessive amounts of data can lead to information overload, regardless of information, and inaccurate decisions (Yigitbasioglu & Velcu, 2012).

Visuals can help extend our short-term memory in two ways. First, a visual compresses a large amount of information. For instance, a set of numbers as well as a line graph are stored as a chunk of information; however, the line graph may contain more information (Few, 2006).

Second, a visual can be an extension of the short-term memory. As visuals are processed quickly, we can regain access to information of a visual in fractions of seconds. This is useful in solving complex problems because a visual can "hold" information while we examine other aspects of a problem (Henderson, 1999). Hence, visuals allow us to process and consider more information, establishing more complex relationships and building more comprehensive frames.

3.2.3 Communication Aids

A visual can aid communication, and, as Wattenberg and Viegas (2008) state, "it gets people talking" (p. 30). This is because visuals are usually made with the intent to convey meaning (Whyte et al., 2008) and to create a shared understanding of available data (Kaplan, 2011; Whyte et al., 2008). War rooms are a classic example for the use of visuals to gain a collective understanding of what is going on (O'Reilly, Bustard, & Morrow, 2005). We will now demonstrate how specific characteristics of visuals can be used in communication and collective sensemaking.

Communication of Complex Relationships

The nonlinearity of visuals enables the communication of complex concepts. For example, verbally explaining the apparently random lines in the exterior design of

Figure 3.5—Frank Gehry's Guggenheim Museum in Bilbao, Spain[9].

Frank Gehry's Guggenheim Museum in Bilbao, Spain (Figure 3.5) would be very challenging. The designing process was heavily supported by computer-aided design (CAD) software, which was developed by the team. The software provided a new visual interface tailored to architectural work. This innovation was recognized as one of the success factors of the Guggenheim Museum project, which was completed on time and on budget (Dodgson, Gann, & Salter, 2005).

Visuals also aid the display of abstract complex concepts, such as objectives and the vision of a project or an organization. In this context, visuals are particularly useful to cope with a portfolio's structural complexity, as they are able to show relationships and options, and hence, enable people to interpret, discuss, and act on them.

For example, a visual called a benefits map can help executives determine gaps between organizational strategies and actions and identify projects that are not aligned with intended strategy (Ward & Daniel, 2005).

Negotiations

Visuals are a powerful artifact for mediating negotiations—they are easier to jointly compile or modify than text. For example, participants in a meeting can

---

[9] Standjourdan, Guggenheim museo, taken on June 26, 2013, retrieved from https://www.flickr.com/photos/stanjourdan/9244901125/ on the 21.07.2015.

alter a visual drawn on a whiteboard, constructing interpretations and solutions together. Visuals also constitute a record of what has been agreed on, in a sense equivalent to meeting notes or a form of short-term memory of what has been discussed.

Research argues how visuals such as Gantt charts mediate negotiations and influence the sensemaking process among various groups of project stakeholders: Gantt charts focus attention on schedule over other aspects of the project. In other words, the visual will encourage negotiations on deadlines, sequences, and durations, but not on, for instance, benefits, resource constraints, scope of the work, conflicting interests, and so on. It is therefore critical for managers to choose visuals consciously, as different visuals steer negotiations in different directions (Yakura, 2002).

Moreover, though some aspects of a visual are negotiable, such as, in the case of the Gantt chart, deadlines, durations, sequence, and tasks, the logic behind visuals is not. For instance, Gantt charts inherently:

- focus on time over other variables;
- are objective (i.e., they present one potential approach to manage work as *the* right way);
- are deterministic (i.e., deviations are seen as errors to be avoided);
- are analytical (i.e., they are based on the idea of breaking down the work in detailed tasks a priori);
- encourage clear individual accountability to specific parts of the project; and
- display tasks as sequential, discouraging iterative work and convergence to solutions.

This logic might not be appropriate for all types and phases of projects. With systematic use, the logic of a Gantt chart becomes embedded in the way projects are managed (Geraldi & Lechler, 2012). Gantt charts are not an exception; actually, all visuals embed a certain logic. Therefore, it is important to unravel the logic behind visuals in order to use them mindfully.

Knowledge

Visuals are not only an artifact for real-time communication, but they can also act as an epistemic object (Nicolini, Mengis, & Swan, 2012), in other words, an object that facilitates the storage and exchange of knowledge (Eppler, 2006; Eppler & Burkhard, 2007; Ewenstein & Whyte, 2009). For example, Toyota has been communicating project information with the help of dense and concise reports that include a short project description and information that ranges from project background and vision to current status (Shook, 2009).[10]

---

[10] See Appendix A for an example of Toyota's A3 report.

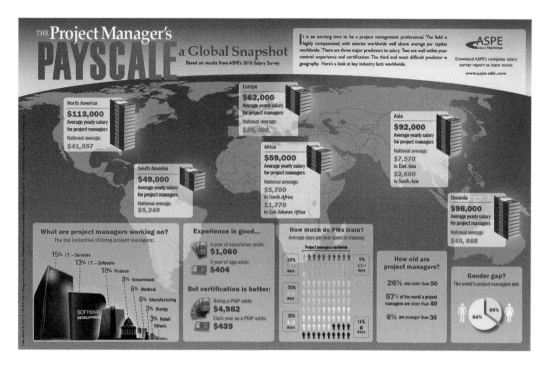

Figure 3.6—Infographic on project managers' payscale. Source: http://www.aspe-sdlc
.com/blog/project-manager-salary-survey-infographic/[11]

Visuals can facilitate the exchange of knowledge in a compressed visual format, for example, through highly condensed dashboards or other infographics, as shown in Figure 3.6.

Emotions

Visuals can create a space for alternative opinions, inspire thinking, challenge stakeholders, trigger change, or convey passion. They also give voice to alternative accounts of a situation (Bell, 2012), as well as space to express frustration, sometimes through humor.

Competing images can also be useful to challenge current realities and plant the seeds of change. They can provide at least some room for passion, individuality, and imagination. Such an intentional use of visuals is particularly relevant to cope with different and contradicting opinions and repression of critical voices. Visuals can therefore help in coping with the socio-political complexity of project portfolios.

Finally, as we communicate through visuals, we are not only providing what is explicitly displayed in the visual, but also constructing an image of organizations and ourselves. This is particularly well recognized and used in marketing (Foss, 2004; McQuarrie & Mick, 1999; Phillips & McQuarrie, 2004). In this respect, visuals are pertinent in project and portfolio contexts, for example,

---

[11] For more infographics in project management, see http://www.pinterest.com/aecfasttrack/project
-management-infographics/.

to increase legitimacy (Justesen & Mouritsen, 2009), to demonstrate capability, and to build a reputation (Meyer et al., 2013).

3.2.4 How Visuals Address Project Portfolio Decision Challenges (Summary)

As demonstrated, visuals support sensemaking and ultimately portfolio decisions by acting as cognitive and communication aids.

By these means, visuals also address portfolio complexity. As cognitive aids they are particularly important for coping with structural and emergent complexities. Based on the notion of structural complexity (see Section 2.2), it becomes apparent that the selection of the optimal portfolio quickly exceeds the cognitive abilities of decision makers. The use of visual aids can be particularly helpful to make complex portfolio problems more accessible. To harness structural complexity demands an understanding of vast amounts of interconnected pieces of information (e.g., interdependencies between projects), different resource types and competencies required for each project, as well as an understanding of the contribution of each individual project and the portfolio as a whole to strategic goals. Visuals can help by displaying each of these perspectives and helping to make sense of the multiple facets of a portfolio. For example, visuals like network diagrams are particularly helpful for understanding independencies among projects. Portfolio visuals in general can also help users grasp and compare the different potential combinations of the project in the portfolio and their impact on portfolio outcomes, for example, potential return, innovation, customer satisfaction, and so on.

Visuals can furthermore play an important role in making the uncertainties of available data visible and more accessible to wider audiences (Spiegelhalter, Pearson, & Short, 2011). Structural complexity makes us often see estimations as deterministic numbers and not probabilities. Displaying uncertainty through well-designed visuals can alert decision makers to the stochastic nature of the data. Forms to display ambiguity are also relevant. Visuals like decision trees help stakeholders understand different portfolio scenarios. Good visuals can also call attention to early signals of problems; they help stakeholders sense and seize cues across different indicators, and allow them to look at data from different perspectives—and encourage people to talk. Finally, visuals can help decision makers grasp contradicting information by encouraging comparisons. In this regard, well-designed visuals and exceptional visual literacy should also help decision makers recognize not only what is available and visible but also the blind spots; as we look mindfully to what is available, we can "see" the missing links, missing perspectives, and so forth, and thereby support addressing not only structural complexity but also the navigation in socio-politically complex situations. By encouraging us to engage with different perspectives, visuals also help us reduce the likelihood of cognitive errors.

A portfolio decision is also a social process, influenced by people's vested interests, which further increase socio-political complexity (see Section 2.4). Visuals can be once again a powerful tool to address complexity and a particularly useful rhetorical device for persuasion: Visuals "are crucial elements for 'mirroring,' as well as 'inventing' reality (Raab, 2008) by using shared symbols for persuasion (e.g., Messaris, 1997) and transporting specific normative ideas behind a veil of seemingly objective representation (Kress & Van Leeuwen, 1996)." (Meyer et al., 2013, p. 494). Furthermore, visuals can serve as boundary objects, which "act as translation and transformation devices across various thought worlds. They make cross-disciplinary work possible" (Nicolini et al., 2012, p. 624). A visual can facilitate the dialogue between different disciplines, cultures, and belief systems, enabling people from different perspectives to communicate and develop a shared understanding of the problem. In simple terms, visuals are a useful communication aid.

In summary, visuals can help sensemaking and influence decisions by:

- Acting as a cognitive aid, because visuals:
  - function as an "initial frame" that anchors the sensemaking process;
  - function as "data" that will initiate further questions and a more elaborate frame (understanding) of the multiple perspectives of portfolio decisions;
  - enable decision makers to more effectively process large amounts of data and solve problems quickly and more accurately;
  - use our natural abilities to recognize patterns;
  - extend the short-term memory, which is otherwise very limited; and
  - are particularly useful for coping with structural, emergent, and behavior complexities.[12]
- Acting as a communication aid, because visuals:
  - help to convey frames and persuade others;
  - mediate and influence the direction of negotiations;
  - act as boundary objects that connect different frames and facilitate the negotiation of meaning, and facilitate convergence to a common understanding;
  - assist communication and collective sensemaking of complex relationships;
  - store and share knowledge and act as a form of organizational memory;
  - inspire thinking, challenge stakeholders, and convey passion to engage or change; and
  - are useful for coping with socio-political complexity, but also partly with behavior and emergent complexities.

3.3 Visuals: Friends or Foes?

Despite all of their benefits, visuals can also influence communication and cognition in a negative, detrimental way.

Visuals can be designed with the intention to deceive readers. For example, Beattie and Jones (1992) studied the annual report of 21 out of the Fortune

---

[12] These insights form the foundations of one of our guiding principles—that visuals are purposeful. In Section 4.6.2 we will return to this argument and propose perspectives for the analysis of portfolio problems.

50 companies and concluded that each report had at least one graphic constructed incorrectly, often with the visible intent to deceive the reader. A classic form of deception is inconsistency in scales. Another study identified that graphs with inconsistent scales led to inferior decisions compared to those that were based on consistent scales. Interestingly, participants in the study did not notice the issue, even after repeating similar tasks five times with incorrectly constructed graphics (Jarvenpaa & Dickson, 1988). This suggests that visuals are powerful instruments and, exactly for this reason, they can be deceiving.

The use of inconsistent scales or other mistakes in visual design may be unintentional, yet the effect remains. Even well-intentioned visuals may confuse and mislead decision makers by providing contradicting, voluminous, ambiguous, unreliable data (Kirschner, Shum, & Carr, 2003).

Possessing visual literacy is an important prerequisite for uncovering potential dishonesty and mistakes in visual design[13] and designing visuals more effectively.

Visual literacy is also relevant to realize the potential benefits of visuals. For example, an advantage of visuals is our improved ability to engage with more data and more perspectives of the problem, leading to enhanced comprehension, and hence, improved decisions. Yet, visuals can have exactly the opposite effect. Lurie and Mason (2007) explored the effect of visual representations in marketing decision making and concluded that "visuals may bias decisions by focusing attention on a limited set of alternatives, increasing the salience and evaluability of less diagnostic information, and encouraging inaccurate comparisons" (p. 160).

Finally, regardless of people's degree of visual literacy, it is important to stress that visuals *are* used, whether mindfully or not. Although we may not know that a 3-D visual of a building looks persuasively "real" and can therefore be used to enhance a construction project's legitimacy, we may still use it. The effect is the same. Thus, the omnipresence of visuals in both personal and work environments explains the need for visual literacy (Eco, 1979; Mitchell, 1994).

Hence, visual literacy is critical for coping with our increasingly visual world in general, as well as aiding portfolio decisions. It moves us from a passive to a mindful engagement with visuals.

3.4   Research Focus

Many types of visuals are currently used in project portfolio management, for example, bubble charts, treemaps, heatmaps, Gantt charts and calendar charts, portfolio funnels, Hoshin Kanri matrices, portfolio tables, roadmaps, network diagrams, efficient frontier graphs, decision trees, and others.[14] Although certain types of visuals recur in the literature and in practice, there is little consciousness about the importance of designing or selecting appropriate visuals for the task at hand.

---

[13] This is discussed in detail in Chapter 4 as we explore the principle "truthful."

[14] See examples in Section 4.6.2.

Yet, project and portfolio managers should engage with visuals in a mindful manner. We have demonstrated how visuals can help or hinder communication and cognition in general and in the project and portfolio decision context in particular. Our research focused on the impact of visuals on individual cognition, and more specifically on decision making. We concentrated on individual cognition in order to first understand how individuals engage with visuals before entering into a more complex context, where groups of people are interacting with visuals. Therefore, the role of visuals as communication aids between individuals is left to further research.

Human cognition involves a variety of mechanisms, including but not limited to memory, problem solving, and decision making (Newell, 1990). In particular, the research focuses on the role of visuals to aid cognition of data and thereby encourages more informed decisions in the project and portfolio management context.

Therefore, from the wide range of perspectives on cognition, our research takes an information process view. From this perspective, one of the most common problems in the cognition of data in complex environments such as portfolio decisions is overconfidence (Klayman, Soll, González-Vallejo, & Barlas, 1999), where engagement with a large amount of data leads to higher confidence but not higher accuracy (Omodei et al., 2005; Tsai, Klayman, & Hastie, 2008). We therefore explore whether this statement holds true for the use of visuals in decisions.

Therefore, our research effort attempted to address the following key question:

How can the use and the design of visuals support cognition of data in project portfolio decisions?

Specifically, our goals have been:

1. to understand the role of visuals in cognition of data in portfolio decisions, and specifically, how visual use and design can influence cognition of data and confidence levels in portfolio decisions; and
2. to enhance visual literacy among practitioners in general, and to develop a critical understanding of the role of visuals in cognition in particular.

While this section focused on *why* visuals are powerful, the next chapter explores *how* visuals can be used and designed. We introduce the concept of visual literacy and our research propositions, which have been empirically tested.

CHAPTER 4

Tapping into the Potential: Visual Literacy

The preceding chapter argued why visuals can be powerful artifacts in the sensemaking process and hence can address portfolio decision challenges. This chapter explores how to exploit their potential, specifically through enhancing visual literacy. This chapter discusses three areas of visual literacy and explores the relationships among them. We introduce propositions that have been tested empirically. The chapter concludes with guiding principles for the design and use of visuals for managers. These principles condense knowledge from data visualization literature and are aimed at informing project and portfolio managers about key aspects of data visualization.

4.1 Visual Literacy

The term *visual literacy* was first coined in 1969 by John Debes and is based on the notion that we can learn to read visuals as we learn to read text (Edwards, 2010). Visual literacy was first introduced in art classrooms, where students learned and interpreted visuals through concepts such as lighting, color, and composition (Baker, 2012). Today, with the omnipresence of visuals, visual literacy has become critical to other disciplines, including project and portfolio management.

At this point, there is no consensus among academics as to what constitutes visual literacy. Table 4.1 summarizes some of the definitions.

Table 4.1—Unraveling the concept of visual literacy.

Concept	Debes (1969)	Bristor and Drake (1994)	Gray (2008)	Brill, Kim, and Branch (2000)	Neri (2001)	Baker (2012)
Group of skills and competencies...	X	X	X	X		X
...to use (understand, interpret, evaluate, learn, think, enjoy)	X	X	X	X		X
...to design (produce, compose, create)			X	X		
...visual messages[15]	X	X				X
...influenced by our experience, interests, emotions, and so on (idiosyncratic, depends on user/designer)					X	

In general, the pertinent definitions suggest that visual literacy entails the following:

- **Use Competency**: knowledge, experience, and skills to understand, interpret, and evaluate visual messages. This includes our ability to learn and think visually, appreciate a visual, and enjoy it.
- **Design Competency**: knowledge, experience, and skills to produce, compose, and create visual messages. This includes our ability to consciously make choices in the design to communicate a certain meaning.

We can acquire these competencies over time as we become increasingly familiar with different types of visuals and their explicit and implicit symbols. We can seek to understand the choices made in the design of visuals and make conscious choices to think and communicate through visuals.

It is not only our visual experience that influences our way of engaging with visuals. Other experiences, emotions, and interests play an important role in how we use and design visuals. Thus, we design and use visuals by leveraging knowledge, experience, and skills that transcend visual literacy, in the same way we write and read text. As a result, visual experiences and visual literacy are idiosyncratic; they depend on the user and designer.

Figure 4.1 displays these three concepts and their interrelationships.

4.2 Design

Chapter 3 demonstrated why visuals influence cognition. For example, the incorrect use of scales in a chart can lead us to see relationships or trends that don't actually exist. Even if the visual design provides a truthful translation from a referent to a visual, the design choices still influence our ability to understand data. Cognitive fit theory suggests that a visual design, which

---

[15] Visual messages can mean several things, including photographs, illustrations, drawings, maps, diagrams, advertisements, and other visual messages and representations, both still and moving. Visual messages are, therefore, related to all we can see (what is visible), and not only visuals (the artifact).

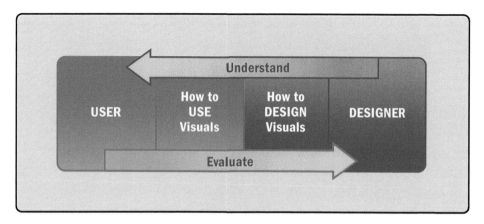

Figure 4.1—Building blocks of visual literacy.

fits the perspective that a person intends to convey, will improve cognition (Jarvenpaa, 1989; Jarvenpaa & Dickson, 1988; Ware, 2012). First, the use of different visual attributes in design, such as position, shape, color, and size, will have an influence on the relative attention given to information, particularly on the early phases of the decision-making process (Jarvenpaa, 1990). Second, because each visual provides a different perspective on the problem, when confronted with two different visuals for the same decision problem (e.g., financial scatter plots versus Gantt charts), managers may approach decision making in different ways (Yau, 2011). It is therefore reasonable to suggest that design—the choice of what and how to display information in a chart—will influence cognition. We therefore propose that the impact of visuals on the cognition of data depends on the *design* of the visuals.

It is not surprising that visual literacy involves the competency to design visuals. We explore how visuals *should* be designed and how their design impacts cognition, as we discuss the principles of visual design in Chapter 5, where specific propositions are elaborated.

4.3 Use

Cognition depends not only on visual design, but also on how visuals are used. Much of what has been written on visual literacy is exactly about developing a critical and informed way of "reading" visuals. We therefore propose that the impact of visuals on cognition of data depends on how visuals are *used*.

It is not an easy task to articulate a general set of recommendations that describe how best to engage with visuals, and even harder to validate them. The way of engaging with visuals is closely related to how we think—in other words, it is idiosyncratic. For example, the effect of visuals in cognition may be independent of whether people engage with visuals in a different order, spend more time with different visuals, or have slightly different interpretations of each visual and use them for different reasons. Therefore, it is reasonable to assume that several yet not all ways of engaging with visuals could lead to similar levels of understanding. Thus, instead of only developing specific and measurable propositions, we ask:

Question 1: How do people use visuals?

We address this question empirically through qualitative analysis and discuss our findings in Chapter 5.

We have specifically investigated the role of visuals as cognition aids in the sensemaking process. In Chapter 3 we proposed that visuals can display different perspectives of a decision problem and hence encourage a more elaborate understanding of a problem. We further argue that there is a complex relationship between the number of visuals used and cognition.

Research suggests that portfolio decisions can be improved through a wise use (Martinsuo & Lehtonen, 2007) of a larger quantity of data (Bourgeois III & Eisenhardt, 1988). Visuals can encourage the use of more data for three reasons: 1) visuals are effective vehicles for understanding a large and complex quantity of data; 2) visuals occupy a similar amount of space in our limited short-term memory, yet, they embed more information; and 3) visuals function as a holding ground, and so they extend our short-term memory.[16] Therefore, the use of multiple visuals enables cognition of even greater quantities of data.

A larger number of visuals can also encourage a wiser use of data. As mentioned above, cognitive fit theory suggests that certain visual designs are more appropriate to show certain perspectives of a problem (Jarvenpaa, 1989; Jarvenpaa & Dickson, 1988; Ware, 2012; Yau, 2011). Hence, if the visuals are purposefully designed,[17] they can display different perspectives of portfolio problems in an effective way. It is reasonable to suggest that decision makers who engage with larger numbers of (purposefully designed) visuals are more likely also to consider different perspectives of the problem.

Yet, more visuals will not necessarily produce better results. Engagement with a larger amount of visuals could lead to information overload. Research suggests that the function describing the relationship between the amount of data analyzed and analytical performance is curvilinear rather than linear: Having more data available is only helpful to a certain extent; thereafter, more data do not lead to a more accurate or better understanding of the situation, yet it increases confidence levels, so people become overconfident but not increasingly correct (Omodei et al., 2005).

If the same amount of data is displayed through different visuals by providing additional perspectives, the redundant display of information may allow a better recognition of trends, patterns, and other insights. In this case, a larger number of visuals would not necessarily lead to information overload.

Yet, the display of different perspectives can require different and more data. For example, the data required to display strategic fit are usually different from

---

[16] These arguments have been explored in detail in Section 3.2.

[17] In Section 4.6.2 we will explain in more detail what we mean by purposefully designed. For now, it is enough to consider it as a design that best shows a certain perspective on a problem.

the data used in scheduling or a stakeholders map. Thus, considering different perspectives can lead to an increase in the amount of information displayed, and hence can lead to information overload. Therefore, we argue that cognition has a curvilinear relationship with the number of visuals used.

Engagement with a large enough number of visuals is not intuitive; actually, it is quite the opposite. Our search for an adequate understanding of a problem (frame) is driven by plausibility, not accuracy; as we find a frame that appears to fit, we are likely not to continue searching for cues (Weick, 1995). We search for satisfactory, not optimal, solutions (Simon, 1955).

Visuals intensify this impulse, "because our minds prefer to take the fastest and easiest route to making a decision, and because images or imagistic texts offer shortcuts toward the endpoint of making a decision, then images . . . will prompt the viewer to make a relatively quick decision, largely ignoring the more analytical, abstract information available in verbal form" (Hill, 2004, p. 33). This is confirmed by Lurie and Mason's (2007) empirical study on marketing decisions, which suggests that visuals restrict rather than increase the amount of information used.

The immediacy of visuals can also make us more vulnerable to cognitive biases, in particular confirmation bias (to favor information that confirms what we believe and to discredit information that shows otherwise [Carroll, 2012]); if a visual strongly supports someone's interests, the person may not engage with other visuals and search for alternative frames. This would suggest that people will tend not to engage with different visuals, and keep with the ones that provide the quickest, easiest, and most convenient understanding of the problem.

Therefore, mindful engagement with more visuals can help people fight against the wish to shortcut the sensemaking process. It would also help reduce cognitive biases, in particular confirmation biases.

Thus, we propose that the use of more visuals would typically encourage decision makers to embrace more perspectives for a "good enough" framing of the problem, without being overwhelmed by them. The use of too few purposeful visuals may indicate a tendency to rash decisions. Using more purposeful visuals would instigate a more elaborate understanding of the problem and hence increased cognition, yet too many visuals can overwhelm as well as lead to overconfidence. Hence, we propose:

Proposition 2a: There is a nonlinear relationship between the number of visuals used and cognition of data.

Visual literacy in use also means choosing *relevant* visuals—visuals that display relevant perspectives and that are more likely to lead to insights. In a portfolio context, this would include those visuals that address typical tasks at hand and help avoid common mistakes in portfolio management.

Overconfidence is another potential result of the engagement with a large quantity of information. Research suggests that the use of more data does not necessarily lead to better decisions, but it does positively impact confidence (Omodei et al., 2005), leading to overconfidence. For example, Tsai et al. (2008) found that when provided with more relevant information, judges became more confident than accurate. Such decision bias is particularly pronounced in more subjective and complex tasks (Klayman et al., 1999) such as a portfolio decision. If this notion also applies to visuals, then it can be expected that the engagement with larger numbers of visuals would increase confidence to a greater degree than cognition, and hence could also contribute to overconfidence. Therefore, we suggest:

> **Proposition 2b: The use of more visuals contributes to an**
> **increase in confidence and can lead to overconfidence.**

4.4   User

Our understanding of visuals is socially constructed; it depends on our cultural background, profession, and the kind of visuals with which we are familiar (Bertin, 1967/2010). Consequently, there is no formula that guarantees the effectiveness of a given visual for all audiences. As argued by Ward, Grinstein, and Keim (2010), "different users, with different backgrounds, perceptual abilities, and preferences, will have differing opinions on each visualization" (p. 26). Therefore, it becomes critical to understand the use and design of visuals in light of the respective user of the visuals, as well as his or her personality, disciplinary, and cultural background (Yigitbasioglu & Velcu, 2012). To address this issue, we explored qualitatively:

> **Question 2: How do people react to different visuals?**

Specifically, we focus on the role of the user in cognition.

Cognition is not only dependent on the design and use of visuals, but also on the visual literacy, experience, professional knowledge, and interests that the user and designer bring to the process. As we argued in Chapter 3, sensemaking, and hence cognition, is influenced by people's own interests, experience, and professional knowledge.

The relationship between cognition and visual literacy and experience is perhaps less intuitive. Given the importance of visuals in the sensemaking process, the visual experiences and visual literacy of a person will also influence cognition. We understand that a careful reader will recognize this is a tautology and hence not a very useful argument. To further elaborate the argument, language is the vehicle of cognition, and so cognition and language are intrinsically related. This means that our cognition can be only as complex as our language skills allow (Geraldi, 1991). Visuals are a type of language (Bell et al., 2014)—actually a very powerful one—as they are different from[18] (Bertin, 1967/2010) and a complement to verbal language in our cognition process. Thus, since language has an impact on cognition and visuals are a form of language, visual literacy—the ability to use visual language and visual experiences (i.e., describing *how* we engage with visual language)—has an impact on cognition.

---

[18] See Chapter 3 for a detailed discussion on visuals as cognitive aids.

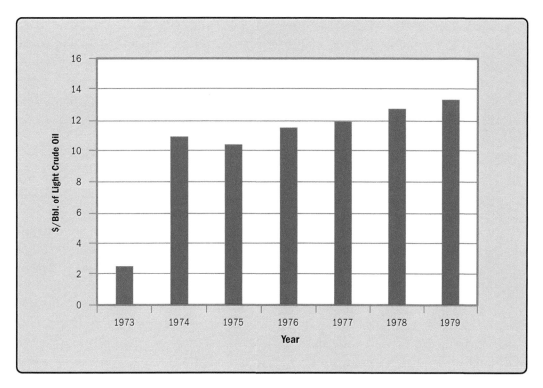

Figure 4.2—Example of a simple bar chart.

The following two examples elucidate this effect. First, understanding how a visual works will help us use it more effectively. An individual who is familiar with the use of logic flow diagrams will be able to interpret Figure 4.2 easily. However, if the person has never seen this type of visual before, he or she will first need to understand that the visual displays relationships between variables and how it does so. Second, knowledge of different types of visuals can help us ask different questions. For example, familiarity with the logic flow visual can help in developing more complex arguments in a more precise and logical manner, and thereby may possibly avoid cognitive errors (Fischhoff, 2006). Third, familiar elements, such as colors, icons, layouts, and styles, can be leveraged to achieve cognitive effects. For example, in U.S. elections, one often sees a reshaping of the U.S. political map. This altered map distorts the familiar visualization of the U.S. map, which represents the exact geographic coordinates of the state borders, to emphasizes a critical data series (number of electoral votes per state) over a less relevant one (shape and aerial surface of each state), and thereby conveys immediate insights into which states may deserve greater campaign attention than others. At the same time, the visual presents a familiar structure, so users will quickly recognize it as a political map of the United States, and will easily locate specific states and interpret their relevance (see, e.g., http://elections .nytimes.com/2012/ratings/electoral-map from *The New York Times*).

We suggest that visual experience influences cognition. A fundamental question remains: How does visual experience influence cognition? The examples above propose three distinct types of influences; however, others exist. Exploring all possible ways in which visual experiences can influence cognition exceeds the scope of this study. We chose to focus on familiarity. Based on the prior conclusion, we argue that familiarity with visuals will make the use of a visual more effective and hence improve cognition, especially when a decision maker has to analyze data under time pressure and cannot afford the time to explore unknown visuals.[19] Moreover, if a person is familiar with different kinds of visuals, he or she can engage with a larger amount of perspectives with greater ease. We therefore suggest:

**Proposition 3a: Cognition is positively influenced
by familiarity with the visuals used.**

Furthermore, familiarity is likely to lead to higher levels of confidence in interpreting a visual accurately. For example, most of us are familiar with a bar chart, and will feel comfortable analyzing Figure 4.2 and stating that the price of light crude oil had a marginal decrease from 1974 to 1975.

Similarly, most project managers are familiar with project S-curves and will immediately recognize project slippage at a point in time (t'), as the actual progress (blue line) trails the target progress (red line), depicted in Figure 4.3. Familiarity with this visual representation will lead to greater confidence in its interpretation, as compared with someone who is confronted with an S-curve for the first time.

Yet, someone who has already experienced the same type of visual previously (even with different data) may recognize different patterns, and may connect the new visual with past experiences and interpretations of a previous project or portfolio decision problem. Such experience is fundamental for a competent evaluation of data. Therefore, we suggest:

**Proposition 3b: Confidence is positively influenced
by familiarity with the visuals used.**

4.5 Relationship Between Visual Literacy Areas

The three areas of visual literacy—use, design, and user—are interdependent. For example, the knowledge about design will inform how users evaluate and use the visuals. The design will also profit from an understanding of how visuals are used, and about how that is influenced by the user. Thus, we propose:

Proposition 4: There is a correlation between design, use, and user.

4.6 Guiding Principles for Visual Design

This chapter summarizes relevant insights on the design of visuals from the literature of data visualization and visual dimension (organization theory),

---

[19] The assessment of this proposition is not straightforward, as this effect needs to be controlled by someone's ability to understand unfamiliar visuals (a type of visual literacy). Yet, it is reasonable to expect that familiarity of visuals will override the ability to understand unfamiliar visuals, because the latter will take more time than the former.

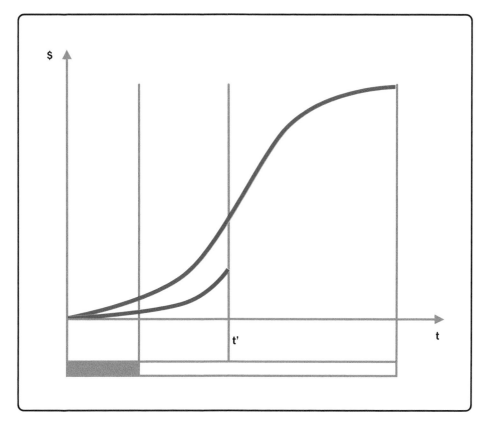

Figure 4.3—Project S-curve.

which we grouped into two core principles: interactive and purposeful, and three supporting principles: truthful, efficient, and aesthetic.

4.6.1 Interactive

This principle constitutes a shift in our understanding of visualization. Visuals are no longer just "static objects, printed on paper or fixed media, modern visualization is a very dynamic process, with the user controlling virtually all stages of the procedure, from data selection and mapping control to color manipulation and view refinement" (Ward et al., 2010, p. 26). Interactivity opens exciting opportunities, moving the focus from producing and disseminating information to interacting with it.

Based on this enhanced understanding, interactive visuals enable users to organize and reorganize data in order to think through and probe ideas, and to access the results of their queries more reliably and confidently (Keim, Kohlhammer, Ellis, & Mansmann, 2010). In this process, visuals allow users to enhance their frames (i.e., their understanding of the problem).[20]

Yet, taking this thinking to an extreme, a white sheet of paper could be considered a starting point to design a visual, where the user has all possibilities to

---

[20] In other words, visuals "melt" into the sensemaking process, as users organize the data according to their emerging questions in the process of framing and reframing, and so decide—within a preestablished structure—which perspectives are relevant.

structure and organize ideas and data. Although it can be useful in several situations, this extreme scenario fails to use data, which is precisely the objective of this research, and therefore will be disregarded.

For this research effort it is useful to consider the degree of visual interaction, from the user's ability to probe and change data within an established visual structure, to the user's ability to completely change the design of the visual itself.

Dashboards constitute a common example of relatively low interaction with visuals, where a user can, for instance, filter or zoom in on specific data sets, yet a bubble chart will remain a bubble chart and will not turn into a pie chart. This approach is useful as it leverages past experience and knowledge on classic portfolio problems. It is also effective, because no time is consumed trying new arrangements and visuals that are familiar to the user, who can quickly spot data patterns (e.g., high risk and high income are always in the corner on the top right of the chart). Finally, it is easier to compare current and past situations or portfolios, which is particularly relevant for portfolio control. The downside is that it does not explore new perspectives, which could be the best fit to address the particularities of a portfolio decision. It can also be a source of systematic biases.

In highly interactive visuals, users explore the raw data through the development of new visuals and/or a combination of visuals. Such situations are often found among data analysts and engineers. Highly interactive visuals allow users to ask new types of questions and leverage their contextual understanding of the specific problem. Such engagement is interesting for some portfolio decisions and problems, particularly unique ones. Yet, use of such visuals is less effective, and can also encourage the user to reinvent the wheel and possibly miss important perspectives because of the complexities involved in portfolio problems.

We therefore, suggest that interaction with the visual is fundamental to the visual's positive impact on cognition. Yet, a mindful user will leverage visuals that allow users to change and organize data and parameters within an established structure—ideally a purposeful one (see the next principle)—and use highly interactive visual tools to design new purposeful visuals when required, to complement existing ones.

4.6.2 Purposeful

The purposeful principle is based on cognitive fit theory, which states that different cognitive tasks can be more effectively displayed by different visuals. For example, a bar chart is adequate for comparisons whereas a scatter plot is suited for analyzing relationships among variables, such as innovation and risk. Table 4.2 provides an overview of these different cognitive tasks.

Cognitive tasks are the basis for our sensemaking process. While questioning and probing our frames—understanding a problem or situation—we are interacting with data (e.g., comparing different parameters, grouping projects around strategic benefits, identifying patterns, exploring relationships and trade-offs, considering interdependencies between projects and resources, etc.). All of these are cognitive tasks that examine the portfolio problem from a different perspective. This is critical because portfolio problems are particularly multifaceted and require the analysis of multiple perspectives.

Table 4.2—Overview of cognitive tasks.

Cognitive Task	Amar, Eagan, and Stasko (2005)	Zhou and Feiner (1998)	Shneiderman (1996)	Yau (2011)	Ward et al. (2010)
Patterns	Characterize distribution			Patterns	Trends
Relationships	Correlate	Composition Associate Correlate Identify	Relate	Relationships	
Spatial Relations				Spatial relations	
Proportions				Proportions	
Differences	Find anomalies			Differences	Anomalies
Grouping	Cluster	Grouping Proximity Similarity Continuity Closure			Clusters
Ranges	Determine range Find extremes				
Ranks	Sort	Sequence			
Focus	Filter Retrieve value Compute Derived value	Attention	Zoom Details on demand Filter in and out		

Therefore, **a visual is purposeful if it addresses at least one relevant perspective of a portfolio problem**. A combination of purposeful visuals will help with the analysis of these multiple perspectives in the portfolio problem.

A fundamental question remains: What are the perspectives that should be visualized in a portfolio problem and how?

Based on typical portfolio management goals and the complexity of most portfolios (see Chapter 2), Table 4.3 presents some relevant perspectives for project portfolio selection.[21]

Perspectives should be developed consciously and tailored for each context. Hence, these are not *the* perspectives to be considered in a portfolio selection decision; instead, they are deemed useful perspectives that address some of the most common issues and embrace common tasks involved in project portfolio selection.

Examples of Purposeful Visuals

We also analyzed current visuals used in portfolio management and decision support systems and looked for the most purposeful ones.[22]

For the purpose of portfolio selection, summary-level project information is typically exhibited in tabular format, which allows the display of numerous

---

[21] Appendix B validates the perspectives suggested above by cross-checking them with the classic steps involved in the selection process.

[22] This analysis is based on four sources of information: 1) literature in portfolio management, in particular Coulon, Ernst, Lichtenthaler, and Vollmoeller (2009); 2) a confidential report on the state of the art in portfolio decision tools; 3) an analysis of the visuals used in portfolio management software based on the Gartner (2013) Reports on BI (Business Intelligence) and PPM (Project Portfolio Management) systems; and 4) other interesting web sources such as http://dashboardspy.com/screenshot-category-all-dashboards.html.

Table 4.3—Perspectives of the portfolio selection process.

Perspectives	Project Portfolio Decision Goals and Complexity	Cognitive Task	Examples of Potential Visuals
Strategic alignment	Ensure alignment between projects and strategic goals	Proportions, relationships, interdependencies, patterns, grouping	Scorecard, dashboard, Hoshin Kanri matrix, strategy map, benefit maps, treemaps, network diagram
Portfolio balancing (Trade-offs)	Recognition and decision of trade-offs in the pursuit of alternative portfolios	Trade-offs, relationships	Scatter plot, bubble chart, treemaps
Thresholds/ Parameters	Consider threshold and parameters (in terms of constraints and/or expected KPIs)	Differences, focus	Heatmap, Chernoff faces, star chart, tables
Interdependencies	Outcome and benefit interdependencies	Interdependencies, grouping	Network diagrams, flow charts, benefit maps
	Time and schedule interdependencies	Trends, patterns, interdependencies	Bar chart (Gantt chart), scatterplot
Choice and scenarios	Do not consider projects in isolation (i.e., one project against the other), but instead consider portfolios (potential combinations of projects) against one another—what are the different *portfolio* options?	Memory of tested frames, decision options	Decision tree, fishbone diagram, mindmap, scatter plot (efficient frontier graph)
Project variety and specific needs	Consider qualitative aspects of each project	Holistic understanding of projects beyond preestablished variables	Condensed visuals (e.g., Infographic)
Risk (Meta-data)	Stochastic nature of future outcomes	Proportions, distributions	Heatmap, histogram, decision tree, pie chart, icon arrays, risk ladders
Lack of available information	Consider not only what is known but where the knowledge gaps are	Patterns, differences, ranges	Scatterplot, star chart, heatmap
Stakeholders	Consider the interests of different stakeholders and their potential influence in projects and portfolio	Relationships, proportions	Network charts, treemap

attributes and the sorting and grouping of projects by one or multiple criteria. Such portfolio tables are popular and useful, as they are intuitive and can provide a high density of information. As illustrated in Figure 4.4, portfolio tables can be augmented with visual attributes to achieve similar effects, as with heatmaps or treemaps (i.e., to allow for the spotting of patterns and outliers).

Figure 4.4—Example of table augmented with visual.

Although portfolio tables may suffice to annotate and display a few simple dependencies, other graphical representations may allow better access to understanding relationships among projects and among their variables.

One of the most commonly found visuals in portfolio management is the portfolio diagram, also known as a bubble chart (Cooper et al., 2001). Bubble charts are often used to graphically represent potential trade-offs between projects in a portfolio and allow selection of a balanced set of projects, by weighing risks against returns, short-term versus long-term contributions, and so forth. There are many different permutations of bubble charts, as additional characteristics of projects can be displayed through the size of the bubble, color, and other attributes.[23]

Some portfolio management and analytics software packages draw on the principles of bubble charts and produce matrices of scatter charts or bubble charts, as exemplified in Figure 4.5. Such representations can be useful in the analysis of trends and the relationship among multiple variables. In a portfolio context, relationships between risk, long- and short-term return, cost, resource usage, innovation, strength of sponsorship, and impact on customer satisfaction could be of interest.

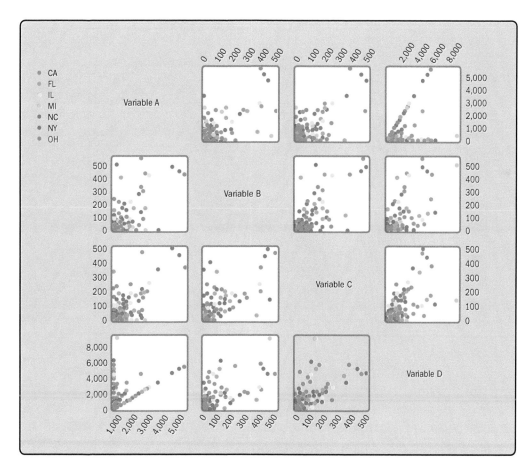

Figure 4.5—Example of a matrix scatterplot.[24]

---

[23] See an example of bubble chart in Figure 4.18.
[24] Source: http://events.pentaho.com/12days-of-Big-Data-Visualizations.html

Treemaps are another purposeful visual for examining balancing large portfolios. Introduced by Johnson and Shneiderman (1991), treemaps divide a rectangle into smaller rectangles, where size, positioning, and color are allowed to reflect various attributes of data. Cable, Ordonez, Chintalapani, and Plainsant (2004) demonstrate the application to portfolio management. In the example in Figure 4.6, projects are clustered by life cycle phase, with attributes of project size (size of the rectangle) and project health (traffic light color code).

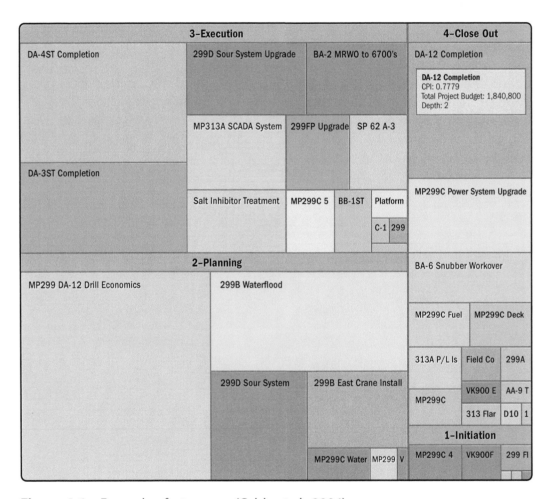

Figure 4.6—Example of a treemap (Cable et al., 2004).

In a similar manner, heatmaps enable decision makers to quickly spot patterns and outliers in large portfolios and thereby help reduce complexity and enable quick insight. Interestingly, heatmaps also allow the retrieval of specific figures when required, as exemplified in Figure 4.7. This is useful, for example, for identifying the lack of knowledge in certain areas or for displaying the stochastic nature of each figure, by making trustworthy figures more visible than first guesses.

Portfolio analysis demands not only an understanding of dependencies among variables, but also among projects, outcomes, benefits, and risks, among others, as explained in Chapter 2.

Roll-out progress for technology deployment (Customer Satisfaction Score)													
Country													
Project / A	B	C	E	F	G	H	I	J	K	L	M	N	O
1 — 3,08	3,40	2,56	3,17	3,18	2,67	3,18	4,13	4,60	3,34	4,26	4,26	3,50	4,27
2 — 3,30	3,06	3,21	2,94	3,08	3,07	3,36	4,45	4,09	4,32	3,90	4,12	4,11	4,53
3 — 2,91	3,33	3,13	2,90	3,62	3,21	3,40	3,86	4,50	4,20	3,85	4,92	4,32	4,61
4 — 3,18	3,23	2,93	3,21	3,73	2,92	3,37	4,27	4,35	3,89	4,32	5,10	3,88	4,55
5 — 3,20	3,57	3,20	3,21	3,87	3,23	3,62	4,30	4,86	4,30	4,32	5,30	4,35	4,92
6 — 3,45	3,50	3,13	3,13	3,47	2,85	3,36	4,68	4,75	4,19	4,19	4,70	3,77	4,55
7 — 3,58	3,64	3,13	3,00	3,50	3,29	3,48	4,88	4,96	4,20	4,00	4,75	4,43	4,72
8 — 2,92	2,56	2,27	2,53	2,76	2,54	2,71	3,88	3,34	2,90	3,29	3,65	3,31	3,57
9 — 3,08	2,88	2,38	2,62	2,83	3,00	2,83	4,12	3,81	3,06	3,43	3,75	4,00	3,75
10 — 3,08	3,07	2,31	2,39	2,89	2,23	2,70	4,12	4,10	2,97	3,08	3,83	2,85	3,54
11 — 2,73	3,27	2,41	2,79	3,06	2,80	2,88	3,59	4,40	3,12	3,69	4,09	3,70	3,82
12 — 2,38	2,69	2,28	2,39	2,56	2,50	2,45	3,08	3,53	2,92	3,08	3,33	3,25	3,18
13 — 3,00	3,13	2,11	2,67	2,94	2,07	2,67	4,00	4,19	2,67	3,50	3,92	2,61	3,50
14 — 3,40	3,29	2,76	3,03	3,25	2,77	3,23	4,60	4,43	3,65	4,04	4,38	3,65	4,34
15 — 3,15	3,20	3,38	3,40	3,31	3,29	3,44	4,23	4,30	4,56	4,60	4,47	4,43	4,66
16 — 3,45	3,57	3,13	3,45	3,50	3,38	3,60	4,68	4,86	4,20	4,68	4,75	4,58	4,90
17 — 3,00	3,47	2,80	3,47	3,18	2,93	3,41	4,00	4,70	3,70	4,70	4,26	3,89	4,61
18 — 3,10	3,21	3,31	3,41	3,53	2,92	3,50	4,15	4,32	4,47	4,61	4,80	3,88	4,75
19 — 2,85	2,75	3,06	3,14	3,28	3,15	3,08	3,77	3,63	4,08	4,21	4,42	4,23	4,12
20 — 2,69	2,60	2,06	2,40	2,94	2,29	2,52	3,54	3,40	2,58	3,10	3,92	2,93	3,28

LEGEND: Dissatisfied — 1 2 3 4 5 — Satisfied

Figure 4.7—Example of a heatmap.

Time dependencies between projects can be easily represented through portfolio Gantt charts (see Figure 4.8), a visual representation that project managers and portfolio decision makers are typically familiar with.

We have also found other, more innovative forms for visualizing schedule interdependencies and time constraints at the portfolio level. The calendar

Task Name	Duration	Predecessors	Schedule
1 Development Accelerator	1 mon		DevTeam 1+2
2 eOrder Application	6 mons	1	DevTeam 1+2
3 eInventory Application	6 mons	1	DevTeam 1+2
4 ePayment Application	6 mons	1	DevTeam 1+2
5 Data Loader	2 mons	2, 3, 4	DevTeam 1+2
6 System Integration	4 mons	2, 3, 4	DevTeam 1+2
7 Pilot Implementation	2 mons	5, 6	DevTeam 1+2
8 Marketing Campaign	6 mons	7	
9 Agile Development Method & Training	1 mon		Coach
10 Office Renovation	12 mons		
11 Server Update	3 mons		HQ-IT
12 Data Conversion Tool	3 mons		HQ-IT
13 Fix of Current Software	6 mons		DevTeam 2+3
14 Enhancement of Current Software	6 mons	13	DevTeam 2+3
15 New Software Testing Method	2 mons		QAEng, Coach
16 Engineering Product Exchange	12 mons		DevTeam 1, 2, or 3

Figure 4.8—Example of a Gantt chart.

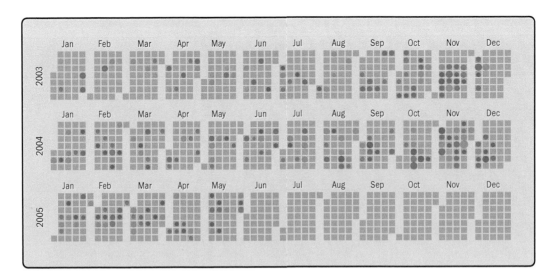

Figure 4.9—Example of an alternative view of schedules.

view (Figure 4.9), for example, is especially suitable for spotting particularly busy periods, where potential resource conflicts may emerge.

Another, less frequently used, yet interesting and very intuitive visual displays the status of projects according to their phase in the project portfolio funnel (Figure 4.10).

Groenveld (1997) suggested the use of roadmaps, displaying the "interaction between products and technologies over time, taking into account both short- and long-term product and technology aspects" (p. 49).

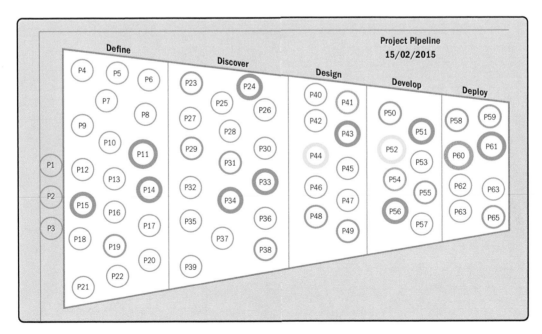

Figure 4.10—Example of project progress displayed according to the portfolio funnel.[25]

---

[25] Source: http://www.enterprisedashboards.com/project-management-dashboard-shows-level-of
-effort-loe-metric/

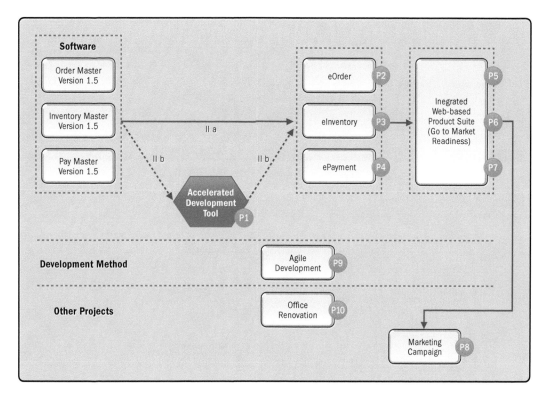

Figure 4.11—Example of a portfolio roadmap (Arlt, 2011).

Figure 4.11 provides an example of such visuals. These kind of visuals are useful for identifying and communicating strategic options.

Network diagrams or "visual project maps" are an option for displaying complex interdependencies, where each network node represents a project, arrows depict the direction of a dependency, and further attributes can be placed on the map, as illustrated in Figure 4.12 (Killen, 2013).

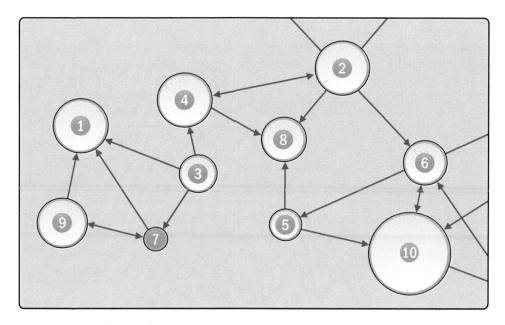

Figure 4.12—Example of a visual project map (Killen, 2013).

The same visual structure can also be used for the display of relationships between stakeholders in the portfolio, the relationship between risks, and so on.

In search of the "optimal" portfolio, project portfolio management has adopted the concept of the "efficient frontier" from financial portfolio management, which represents all optimal solutions (Markowitz, 1952), whereas all other portfolio combinations (i.e., those below the efficient frontier) are deemed suboptimal (Figure 4.13). Although portfolio management tools often contain this representation, it is of limited value for practical portfolio selection decisions, because decision-relevant values can be easily displayed in other representations, such as in portfolio tables. Yet, as structural complexity increases, such visuals can be of value.[26]

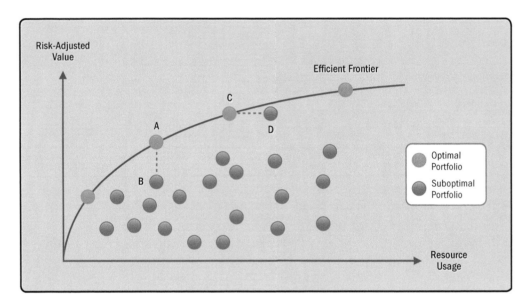

Figure 4.13—Example of a visualization of an efficient frontier (Arlt, 2010, p. 107).

Decision trees can be useful for evaluating a set of binary strategic options. They can also be used to analyze the impact of risk on the project, program, and portfolio levels. Figure 4.14 shows an example of an augmented decision tree for a scenario analysis.

There are many other types of visuals that can be purposeful in the context of portfolio decisions. Lengler and Eppler (2007) have developed a comprehensive overview of the different types of visuals available for representation of abstract ideas, and their different classifications. The overview was visualized as a periodic table—a purposeful visual in itself that takes advantage of our familiarity with the periodic table of chemical elements.

---

[26] The "efficient frontier" representation reduces the portfolio decision to the trade-off between two variables. It is, however, necessary to consider multiple relevant variables. Therefore, this visual alone would be insufficient to select the optimal portfolio and would require the use of more visuals that represent other perspectives.

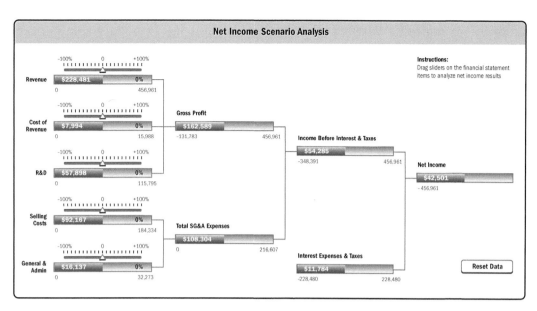

Figure 4.14—Example of a decision tree.[27]

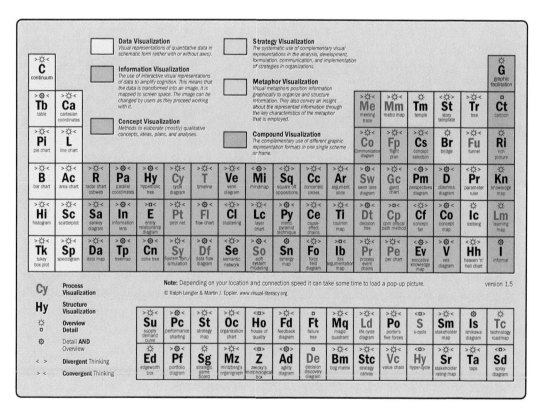

Figure 4.15—Periodic table of visualization methods (Lengler & Eppler, 2007).
Source: http://www.visual-literacy.org/periodic_table/periodic_table.html

_____

[27] Source: www.microstrategy.com/DashboardGallery/Dashboards/IncomeStatementSilver.asp

4.6.3 Supporting Principles

Though the principles "interactive" and "purposeful" are contextual and require an understanding of portfolio decision challenges, the supporting principles are generally applicable to any context and represent generic principles of visual design.

(1) Truthful

Visuals are powerful tools of persuasion and therefore can also potentially mislead and deceive. Much of this power lies in the translation process from data into visuals.

As explained in Section 3.2, the design of visuals inevitably involves a translation from data, concepts, and ideas (i.e., the referent) to a physical representation (the visual). The referent is what visuals represent (Pauwels, 2006). For example, a Gantt chart represents tasks, their duration, and interdependencies. What is represented and how it is represented is a choice that will affect what is most salient in the visual, the legitimacy it conveys, and so forth. A visual is never neutral.

If visuals serve the purpose to support cognition and informed decisions, they should be truthful and strive for a factual and accurate display of the relevant data. A set of visuals should be used to present all decision-relevant perspectives and not only those that may support a unilateral point of view.

In order to enhance our ability to design and use truthful visuals, it is important to understand the ways in which visuals may be deceptive and both recognize such deceptions when we are presented with visuals and avoid them when we are designing visual representations. From the data visualization literature we have identified three properties of visual representations of data that may be deceiving.

Data Quality

"Graphics reveal data" (Tufte, 2001, p. 13), and thus can only be as good as the data they represent. This is particularly challenging in project and portfolio contexts, as the maturity of project management information systems and degree of data accuracy are uneven at best, as a result of the complexity of the context. Data should be relevant, accurate, and timely (Arlt, 2010). By timely, we mean the following:

- Because conditions change constantly and projects evolve, data need to be updated frequently to allow for informed decisions. Such timing often constitutes a practical challenge in project management, for example, project key performance indicators (KPIs) are not always compiled and escalated early enough, which may lead to uninformed or delayed decisions.
- As projects develop, the relevance of a particular KPI may change. For example, changes in the project context may make a KPI less important

and require one or multiple new KPIs that will more accurately capture the progress and status of projects and programs in the portfolio (see the discussion in Maylor, Geraldi, Johnson and Turner, 2009).

Moreover, managers need to ensure that the relevant data for portfolio decisions are collected and available, which means using metrics that best support the decision-making process. Inadequate metrics that do not "fit" the decision context may lead to erroneous conclusions and decisions and suboptimal portfolios, regardless of how the data are presented and processed.

In addition to the availability of high-quality data, it is important that information for all projects is available (Blichfeldt & Eskerod, 2008) and that the project information is comparable. Otherwise, projects will not undergo the same consistent and rigorous filtering, selection, and review process. A potential consequence of poor and incomplete data is the misallocation of resources, as well as resource scarcity, and finally, suboptimal portfolio choices.

Misinterpreting Visuals

Visuals can be misunderstood. Although, ideally, visuals are intuitively understood by anyone regardless of individual prerequisites, a degree of visual literacy in the subject matter is typically required. For example, portfolio decision makers should be comfortable with the use of Gantt charts from managing projects and should know how to use other typical representations of portfolio data, such as bubble charts and treemaps.

However, portfolio decisions involve a diverse spectrum of contributors, influencers, advisors, and decision makers. Adequate labels and explanations can be crucial for avoiding misunderstandings. Even within a narrow domain, misleading labels can lead to unnecessary confusion. For example, the unit of time is unclear in the example in Figure 4.16a. Figure 4.16b, in contrast, provides a combination of visual and tabular information to communicate more clearly.

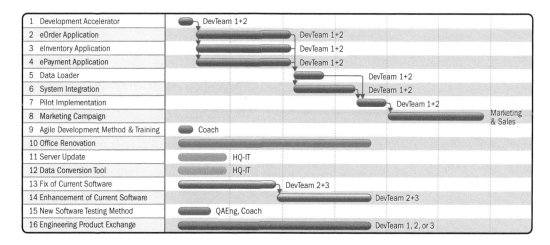

Figure 4.16a—Gantt chart example without a time scale.

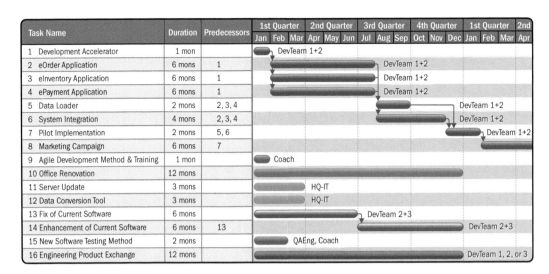

Task Name	Duration	Predecessors	1st Quarter			2nd Quarter			3rd Quarter			4th Quarter			1st Quarter			2nd
			Jan	Feb	Mar	Apr	May	Jun	Jul	Aug	Sep	Oct	Nov	Dec	Jan	Feb	Mar	Apr
1 Development Accelerator	1 mon		DevTeam 1+2															
2 eOrder Application	6 mons	1									DevTeam 1+2							
3 eInventory Application	6 mons	1									DevTeam 1+2							
4 ePayment Application	6 mons	1									DevTeam 1+2							
5 Data Loader	2 mons	2, 3, 4												DevTeam 1+2				
6 System Integration	4 mons	2, 3, 4												DevTeam 1+2				
7 Pilot Implementation	2 mons	5, 6													DevTeam 1+2			
8 Marketing Campaign	6 mons	7																
9 Agile Development Method & Training	1 mon		Coach															
10 Office Renovation	12 mons																	
11 Server Update	3 mons					HQ-IT												
12 Data Conversion Tool	3 mons					HQ-IT												
13 Fix of Current Software	6 mons									DevTeam 2+3								
14 Enhancement of Current Software	6 mons	13												DevTeam 2+3				
15 New Software Testing Method	2 mons			QAEng, Coach														
16 Engineering Product Exchange	12 mons													DevTeam 1, 2, or 3				

Figure 4.16b—Gantt chart example with a time scale.

Tufte (2001) suggests: "Clear, detailed and thorough labeling should be used to defeat graphical distortion and ambiguity. Write out explanations of the data on the graphic itself. Label important events in the data" (p. 77).

At first sight, Tufte's suggestions seem obvious, yet in practice they are often ignored, with misunderstandings and false interpretations of visual resulting.

Persuasion "Tricks"

Portfolio decisions can be highly political and may lead to changes in power and influence of individuals and stakeholder groups. Visuals may be created—intentionally or unintentionally—to support the argument of an individual or a group, instead of providing an unbiased and factual depiction of a situation. Visuals thereby can become political or argumentative instruments (Beattie & Jones, 1992; Lurie & Mason, 2007). In most situations it would be naïve to think that we are dealing with neutral visuals, solely serving the purpose of truthfully describing data. Instead, it may be more useful and realistic to accept that portfolio decisions—like most group decisions—are a learning, negotiation, and bargaining process (Kester, Griffin, Hultink, & Lauche, 2011; Martinsuo, 2013). Accepting this reality helps users critically engage with visuals instead of blindly trusting them as a truthful mirror of reality.

Filtering

Choosing what information to display influences visuals the most. In most scenarios, we cannot display every dimension of a project. As a result of such information overload we wouldn't understand anything, so it is necessary to choose a manageable subset of relevant data.

Such a choice, however, will affect decisions. Lurie and Mason's (2007) study on the effect of visual representations on marketing decisions identifies some of the consequences of filtering. The study concludes that "[a]lthough visual representations are likely to improve marketing manager efficiency, offer new insights, and increase customer satisfaction and loyalty, they may also bias decisions by focusing attention on a limited set of alternatives, increasing the salience and evaluability of less diagnostic information, and encouraging inaccurate comparisons" (Lurie & Mason, 2007, p. 160).

It is reasonable to suggest that the same logic would apply to project portfolio decisions. Projects would be represented by—and their status reduced to—certain KPIs, which could be graphically displayed. This could potentially limit the understanding of the project and drive behavior accordingly. Some KPIs can be more easily recorded than others, such as qualitative characteristics of projects, which will be less likely to be translated into visuals for that reason.

Deliberate Deception

Visuals can also be deliberately manipulated to deceive audiences. The book *How to Lie with Statistics*, authored by Darrell Huff in 1954, was the first to call attention to some of the typical ways of deceiving with visuals, such as changing scale and displaying one-dimensional data in two- or three-dimensional charts. Tufte (2001) introduced the concept of the "lie factor" of a visual, describing it as the ratio between the size of the effect as shown in a graphic to the size of the effect in the data.

Many examples of intentional or unintentional distortion in visuals can be found in practice. Most notably, a bulk of financial accounting literature studied measurement distortions in corporate annual reports and prospectuses. A review of many of these studies suggests that graphic distortion ranges from 24% to 68% of graphics, with a mean level of measurement distortion from 13% to 86% (Beattie & Jones, 2002).

Previous research also suggests that we are susceptible to deceptions and do not recognize them easily. An experimental study identified that graphs with inconsistent scales led to inferior decisions compared to those based on consistent scales. Furthermore, the participant did not notice that graphs had inconsistent scales even after repeating similar tasks five times (Jarvenpaa & Dickson, 1988). This shows that managers need to be more aware of those tricks, to recognize them and avoid deception both in use and design.

Creating Different Emphasis

Visuals can be used to attract the emphasis or focus of an audience to certain aspects of the portfolio problem, because different visual structures will emphasize different facets of data and display them within a distinctive logic.

For example, using a schedule in Gantt chart format is likely to shape the questions that one would raise about the project, such as "Why is Task A not progressing as planned?" or "What is a realistic duration of the task and how will this delay impact our on-time delivery?" (Yakura, 2002). Though such questions may be relevant in a generic project context, they might not be useful or effective in certain scenarios (e.g., for accelerating the progress of an iterative project) where task interdependencies are not limited to input and output at the beginning and end of a task.

As explained in Section 3.2, the logic that is embedded in a visual acts as a boundary in the negotiation of meaning and directs attention to a specific aspect of a decision task, hence channeling the sensemaking process accordingly. Therefore, it is critical for managers to choose visuals consciously, because different visuals may drive conversations and negotiations in different directions.

Congruence Between the Nature of the Visual and the Nature of Data

Another aspect of persuasion through visuals lies in the conscious use of a mismatch between the nature of the data and the nature of its visual representation. This would include, for instance, the design of visuals that display data as if they would be more precise, accurate, objective, and certain than they really are.

For example, the precise display of imprecise data constrains project flexibility but evokes legitimacy. Such a trick is often used in projects. For example, a Gantt chart displays uncertain information about a project's future through an objective visual and implies that the bars represent an objective (and precise) description of project tasks, their sequence, and duration (Geraldi & Lechler, 2012; Yakura, 2002). Three-dimensional renderings of a future building produced in the early stages of the project yield similar effects. They act as customers' promises, and borrow the legitimacy of the photo to make the uncertain future look like a concrete reality (Justesen & Mouritsen, 2009). The handmade sketches used in an engineering office attempt the opposite, that is, to show that the design was still not clearly defined and will be maturing during the course of the project.[28]

Likewise, stochastic data are often represented by data points instead of ranges, subject choices as objective realities, ambiguous data as unambiguous, and so on. Therefore, one should be mindful of the congruence between the nature of the visual and the nature of the data, and its implied meanings.

(2) Efficient

This principle is based on how visuals can help us cope with our limited short-term memory, with our difficulty holding large amounts of information in our brain while analyzing a complex problem. Efficient visuals take advantage of our natural ability to interpret them. They display the maximum amount of information in the smallest space possible, so that the visual can be processed rapidly and accurately. Four tips for developing efficient visuals from data visualization literature are summarized below.

A) Utilize Natural Visual Skills

As mentioned in Section 3.2, natural visual skills help us discern certain patterns, but not others. The first serious attempt to understand these patterns was undertaken by the German Gestalt school of psychology, which dates back

---

[28] Based on conversations with an engineering consulting firm.

Table 4.4—Rapidly recognizable visual features, based on Few (2006) and Healey (2012).

Principles	Definition	Illustration	Examples of Application in Data Visualization
Proximity	We perceive objects that are located near one another as part of a group		Grouping values or projects guides viewers to scan a series of visuals in a specific direction
Closure	We perceive open, incomplete structures as closed and complete		Use this to increase the data/ink ratio, increasing the efficiency of the visual
Similarity	We perceive similar objects as part of a group		Use similar color, shape, or orientation to group values in a graphic, such as data on R&D projects as a triangle and on IT as a circle
Difference	We recognize a different object easily if it has different color (hue), intensity, orientation, length, size, curvature, shadow, or motion		Use different features to call for anomalies, or problems, such as a different color for projects not progressing as planned
Continuity	We perceive aligned objects as part of a group		Hierarchical structure of bullet points
Enclosure	We perceive objects that are confined within a border as part of a group		Highlight grouping of projects or values by circling them
Connection	We perceived connected objects as part of a group		Represent organizational processes, project interdependencies, and so forth

to 1912. The school developed the Gestalt laws, which are still recognized today (Ware, 2012).[29] Much useful research exists in the area, such as pre-attentive processes of visual cognition (Healey, 2012), that is, the unconscious process of detecting basic features of visual objects and discerning what's important. Ware (2012) provides a comprehensive and dense summary of the developments in this area. Table 4.4 summarizes Gestalt laws and pre-attentive processing patterns.[30]

The examples below illustrate how some of these patterns can help address project portfolio decision complexity.

Example 1: Coping with structural complexity by grouping similar projects:

The visual recognition of groups of projects with identical or similar characteristics can help in dealing with large numbers of projects in a portfolio. Decision

---

[29] The Gestalt laws still constitute the building blocks of most current literature in the area, although the neural mechanisms proposed by the school have been falsified.

[30] It was believed that the first stage preceded attention—therefore, the term *pre-attentive*—and that one could only recognize the patterns described in Table 4.3. There were some things that could be seen, and others that couldn't. Today, we know that this is not the case. We learned that our visual process is purposeful; we do not attempt to re-create an accurate image of what we see in our brain. Instead, we capture only what we perceive to be relevant for our current task (Healey, 2012), and we can capture any information if we focus on it. Thus, the role of attention in vision is far more prominent than expected in the past, and the patterns described in Table 4.3 are not as relevant as we used to think. Yet, it is still true that our visual cognition is empowered if we follow these principles.

makers can identify clusters by looking at the proximity of projects across different dimensions of a portfolio, such as innovation, degree of commercial impact, investment, project type, risk, or strategic objective. Figure 4.17 illustrates how the uses of attributes such as color, size, and proximity in a bubble chart help differentiate and group projects.

Example 2: Coping with emergence by controlling changes and identifying early warning signals:

Using our natural ability to spot differences and similarities is a particularly powerful feature of human visual cognition that helps us recognize changes in a portfolio. If, for example, deviations are marked in a different color, we can quickly identify them even when confronted with data for a large number of projects. Figure 4.7 shows a simple example of a heatmap for how 20 ongoing projects are performing according to different criteria. Green and red areas immediately attract attention for a large set of data that can be displayed in a very compressed form. Recognizing the same pattern in a scatterplot, for example, would have been much harder, if not impossible.

Human visual cognition does not enable an equal understanding of all pattern types. For example, we are much less able to compare two-dimensional areas—and particularly angles—accurately. This means that pie charts are usually an inefficient display of quantities and position along a common scale. Similarly, star charts (also called spider diagrams) or radar charts, when used

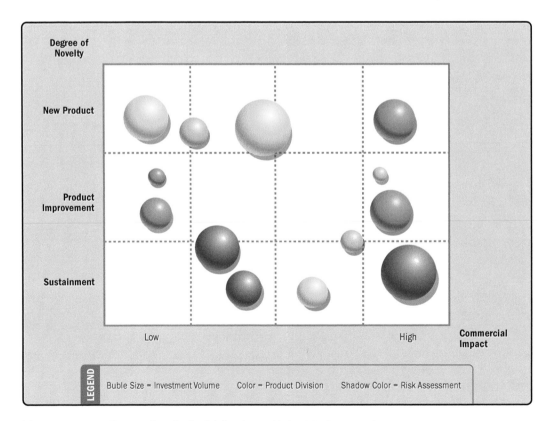

Figure 4.17—Example of a bubble chart (Arlt, 2010, p.119).

on their own, are often inefficient. Due to their circular shape actually obscures data, they make comparisons more laborious and do not display data accurately.[31] In both cases, a simple bar chart is better suited (Few, 2006).

Yet, two-dimensional representations can also be efficient if used mindfully. For example, the use of multiple spider diagrams with each representing a project can be useful for spotting differences between projects. In this case, the visual will draw on our ability to discern shapes rather than 2-D areas. Pie charts lead to accurate judgments of proportions of the whole (Simkin & Hastie, 1987), particularly of compound proportions (A+B versus C+D) (Spence & Lewandowsky, 1991). Another key advantage of pie charts is familiarity: Everyone recognizes that the slices are part of a whole (Spence, 2005). Similarly, most portfolio visuals that utilize bubble charts represent required investment through the size of the bubbles, thereby using surface area to represent quantities. Such visualization is only adequate to provide an overview of the range of project sizes in the portfolio and to discern significantly different project sizes intuitively and rapidly. It is not suitable to discern projects with similar sizes.

Thus, efficient visuals will utilize natural visual cognitive skills mindfully, and often in combination.

B) Mindful Use of Space

As mentioned above, efficient visuals convey the largest amount of information in the smallest space. It is meaningful to increase the size of a portfolio dashboard through, for example, the use of large whiteboards, projectors, or high-resolution or multiple monitors, which allows for a quicker switch between visuals and an increased performance in processing visual information. Yet, we have a limited visual angle that allows us to simultaneously process visual information at a particular moment. Our information processing ability increases the more we can capture in each view. Due to our limited short-term memory, it is useful to place the largest amount of information in that space. If visuals "fit" into our visual angle, we can revisit them rapidly and information is exchanged in and out of the short-term memory rapidly; hence, information is processed more easily. As a consequence, a wise use of space will improve the efficiency of a visual.

This insight leads to the consideration of the data-ink ratio, that is, the amount of data displayed with the amount of ink used to display a graphic (Tufte, 2001). As computer technology, and especially display and graphics processing power, has developed dramatically in the last decades, virtually anyone can develop complex graphics. Visual skills and mindfulness have not kept pace with these developments, and as a result, inadequate choices

---

[31] Star charts can be useful, for instance, to explore trends and differences across several star charts and not within one. For example, 30 projects, each represented in a star chart, can provide such an effect. The goal is not to compare specific dimensions within a project, but to look at patterns across them. In this case, we profit from our natural ability to recognize distinct shapes, not to compare 2-D areas.

are made, which neither fully utilize the potential of visuals, nor utilize our natural visual cognition abilities. For example, most users of PC spreadsheet applications are familiar with the use of 3-D bar charts; however, the third dimension of a bar chart does not add any additional content, but constitutes a visual effect without purpose (see the difference between Figure 4.18a and Figure 4.18b). Such "chart junk" may confuse the user and increase processing time and is inefficient, as a dimension is introduced but is misused.

Visual use and design can be improved by doing the following (Tufte, 2001):

- Eliminating chart junk, that is, any unnecessary elements of the chart, such as unintentional optical art (e.g., moiré vibration—stripes used in bar graphs), unnecessary grid lines, or self-promoting design elements, such as unnecessary use of colors (3-D in a 2-D graphic, meaningless imagery, frames, etc.).

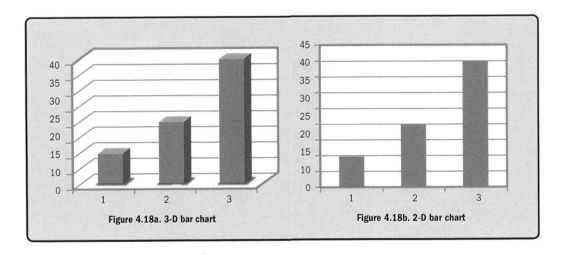

Figure 4.18a. 3-D bar chart   Figure 4.18b. 2-D bar chart

- Erasing non-data-ink (ink that does not represent relevant data), within reason. See, for example, Figure 4.19.

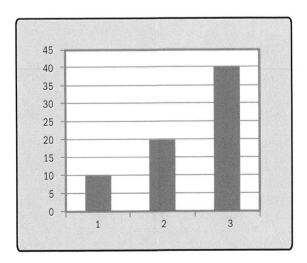

Figure 4.19—Conventional bar chart.

- Erasing redundant data-ink, within reason. See, for example, Figure 4.20.   **57**

Tapping into the Potential

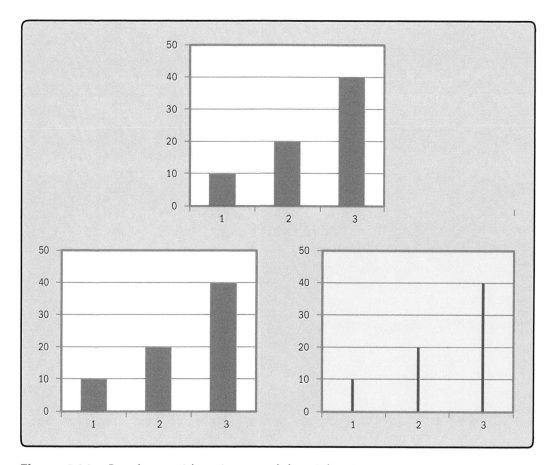

Figure 4.20—Bar charts with an increased data-ink ratio.

- Using multifunctioning graphical elements—an element represents data and performs a design function (e.g., data-based grids).

C) Combine Different Purposes in One Visual, When Possible

The combination of visuals should be done in a mindful way and should include as many visuals as necessary to display all relevant perspectives for a project portfolio decision. Yet, this is likely to lead to a variety of visuals. This variety can be problematic; the human brain requires a time period to "set up" when changing from one type of visual representation to another, hence, variety reduces efficiency in data cognition. Thus, one needs to trade off the necessary variety for a holistic understanding of the data with the need for a consistent and concise dashboard to enhance the efficiency of visuals.

D) Use Redundancy Mindfully

A potential approach to display a variety of perspectives in an efficient manner is the mindful use of redundancy. The provision of intentionally redundant

Group of Projects	Long Term 2014-2019			Short Term FY 2014		
	Return ($)	Cost ($)	ROI (%)	Return ($)	Cost ($)	ROI (%)
1 Development Accelerator	390,000	200,000	195%	325,000	100,000	325%
2 eOrder Application Development	5,000,000	2,500,000	200%	250,000	2,000,000	13%
3 eInventory Application Development	1,500,000	750,000	200%	75,000	700,000	11%
4 ePayment Application Development	1,500,000	600,000	250%	75,000	500,000	15%
5 Data Loader Development	300,000	50,000	600%	0	50,000	0%
6 System Integration	400,000	150,000	267%	0	150,000	0%
7 Pilot Implementation	30,000	300,000	10%	30,000	300,000	10%
8 Marketing Campaign	1,000,000	500,000	200%	0	500,000	0%
9 Agile Development Training	100,000	150,000	67%	20,000	150,000	13%
X 10 Office Renovation	0	5,000,000	0%	0	1,000,000	0%
1 11* Server Update	0	250,000	0%	0	250,000	0%
1 12* Data Conversion Tool	0	100,000	0%	0	100,000	0%
13 Fix of Current Software	1,500,000	1,000,000	150%	300,000	1,000,000	30%
14 Enhancement of Current Software	2,800,000	3,000,000	93%	560,000	3,000,000	19%
15 Improved Software Testing Method	50,000	100,000	50%	10,000	100,000	10%
16 Engineering Product Exchange	10,000,000	500,000	2000%	0	500,000	0%

*Mandatory Projects

Total	0	350,000		0	350,000	
Goals / Constraints	Goal	350,000		Goal	1,200,000	4,500,000 Limit

Figure 4.21—Example of approaches to improve readability.

information through placement and color, label, and size helps the reader to differentiate, perceive, and learn more quickly and easily than single encodings (Rams, 2013).

Figure 4.21 displays a small pipeline of candidate projects and demonstrates the application of such aesthetic principles and guidelines to portfolio selection and how aesthetic design supports the objective of purposeful visuals. Combined and intentionally redundant data and graphs allow easy scanning of attributes describing the returns and costs of candidate projects in a portfolio, as well as the read-out of exact data. Subtle shading of alternating rows enables better readability of data, and colors emphasize critical values and selected projects.

(2) Aesthetically Pleasant

Whether intentional or not, there is an aesthetic aspect to all visualizations (Arnheim, 1954). A visual is aesthetic if it is perceived as harmonious, professional, and beautiful. Traditionally, designs would trade between functionality and aesthetics (Lau & Moere, 2007). Today, accomplished designers have acknowledged the importance of aesthetics as integral to the usefulness of an object and recognized the impact beautiful design has on people (Rams, 2013).

Aesthetic elements can and should be more than merely decorative, since they can increase the utility of a visual representation. For example, as shown in the Sankey diagram illustrated in Figure 4.22, magnitude of funding is represented by both numbers and width of the flows and can therefore be recognized much easier than in a mere tabular format. Color further distinguishes different funding sources that are also grouped and labeled.

Tufte (2001) proposes several guidelines for aesthetic design, including the proper choice of format and design; the combined used of words, numbers, and drawings; a sense of relevant scale; and the avoidance of superfluous decorative elements.

It goes beyond the objective of this section to explain how to make aesthetic visuals, as 1) there is no agreement among designers as to what those factors are, and 2) aesthetics is contextual and idiosyncratic.

What is important for us is to establish the importance of aesthetics, as well as to improve cognition in portfolio decisions. The relationship between aesthetics and cognition is less intuitive and probably weaker than the other principles, yet still relevant.

Other management areas and studies have previously indicated the importance of aesthetics. For example, studies on working space have suggested that people enjoy working in an aesthetically pleasant context. They are even more likely to feel at home or enjoy staying at work. One of the most well known and empirically tested understandings of service quality, ServQual, proposes aesthetics as one of its 10 elements[32] (Parasuraman, Berry, & Zeithaml, 1991; Parasuraman, Zeithaml, & Berry, 1988), in particular because aesthetics

---

[32] The element referring to aesthetics is termed *tangibles* and defined it as the appearance of physical facilities, equipment, personnel, and communication materials.

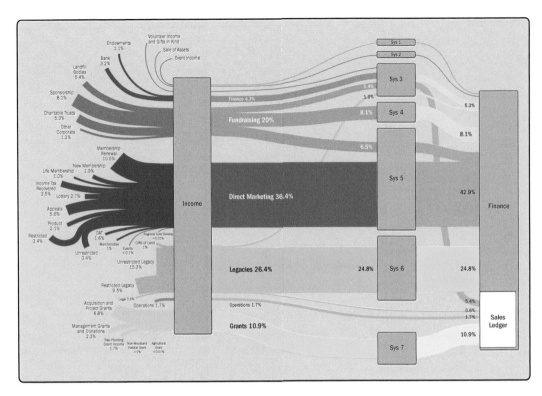

Figure 4.22—Woodland Trust Income Portfolio. Source: www.visguy.com/2009/10/26/follow-the-money-visio-sankey-diagram/

evoke legitimacy and professionalism. Similarly, it is reasonable to expect that aesthetics will also influence portfolio contexts for the same reasons—well-being and impression of legitimacy and professionalism. If people enjoy working with aesthetic visuals, they are likely to spend more time and energy with them; they may also trust aesthetically pleasant visuals more because they feel the visuals are professional and legitimate.

4.7 Concluding Notes

Based on the discussion above, we suggest:

> **Proposition 1a: Cognition of data is positively influenced by adherence to design principles (interactive, purposeful, and supporting).**

With an increase in cognition, decision confidence—the feeling of having done something correctly (Insabato, Pannunzi, Rolls, & Deco, 2010)—is also expected to increase. Therefore, we propose:

> **Proposition 1b: Confidence is positively influenced by adherence to design principles (interactive, purposeful, and supporting).**

Resistance to change is commonly experienced in organizations, and we should not expect any different from the introduction of new visuals. People get used to certain tools and visuals and are challenged or reluctant to "see" a problem from a different perspective, even if such new perspective will be beneficial. Therefore, we would like to understand the role of change in visual design and its impact on cognition. Would resistance to change lead to lower cognition, even if the new visual is designed better? We therefore suggest:

Proposition 1c: Despite negative implications of change (e.g., adoption problems, learning curve), improvement on visual design positively impacts cognition of data.

Finally, before we conclude this chapter, it is important to emphasize that we attempted to develop generic guiding principles that would be applicable across a wide range of portfolios. Yet, we do not suggest that visuals designed for one context would be automatically applicable to others. On the contrary, the principle of purposeful design and use of visuals states that visuals need to display the different and relevant perspectives of the specific problem at hand. As problems and related decision tasks change, so do the perspectives and hence the visuals to be used.

CHAPTER 5

Research Design

5.1 Methodological Challenges

Studying project portfolio decisions is challenging:

(1) Gaining access to boardroom portfolio decisions is difficult, as they are often confidential and closely guarded.

(2) Portfolio decisions do not take place at one moment in time, at one level of the organization, and in one singular location. Hence, behavior in decision situations is not easily studied.

(3) Research often aims to improve decision quality, which is difficult to measure (Dean & Sharfman, 1996). Because portfolio decisions are made under uncertainty and based on incomplete and widely distributed information, there is no definitively "best" decision. Even a post-factum analysis of a decision would not be sufficient to judge decision quality, as it could not provide information on outcomes of alternative decisions and is often influenced by hindsight bias. Moreover, what constitutes the "best decision" varies across different stakeholders and interest groups. Hence, it is hard to measure the dependent variable (decision quality).

(4) There are so many variables playing a significant role in portfolio decisions that it is nearly impossible to single out the influence of an element in the decision, in this case, the visuals and how they have been used.

Given our research objective and focus on the impact of visuals in individual cognition instead of complex group decisions in organizational settings, we have opted for a human subject experiment.

In an experimental setup, it was possible to control for the three most influential factors in individual decisions, namely, decision features, situational factors, and individual differences (Appelt, Milch, Handgraaf, & Weber, 2011). Situational factors and decision features were constant throughout our careful design of the experimental scenario, decision task, and laboratory conditions. The variables were the visuals (our independent variable) and individual differences. We controlled for individual differences through measurement of the subject's decision-making competence (level of confidence and analytical thinking), based on Bruine de Bruin, Parker, and Fischhoff (2007), and demographics.

Despite its limitations, experimental research is a useful methodology to approach certain types of questions, in particular to delve into specific aspects of individual and group behavior, which are useful to inform and complement management and organization studies. Yet, although examples of experimental research on decision making abound, particularly in psychology and behavior economics, there is scant work based on experiments in project management. There are noteworthy exceptions (e.g., Arlt, 2010; Gersick, 1988; Harrison & Harrell, 1993; and Killen, 2013). We join their effort to bring experimental research to project management research.

5.2 Experimental Rational

The objective of the experiment was to test the influence of visual design, use (number of visuals), and user (familiarity with visuals used) on cognition, and then explore how these relationships are affected by an improvement in visual design.

Visual design refers to whether the visuals adhere to the design principles proposed in Section 4.6, namely whether they are interactive, purposeful, and include the supporting principles (truthful, efficient, and aesthetic). We developed three dashboards adhering to these three guiding principles, and a fourth dashboard that does not follow any of the principles. Table 5.1 provides an overview of the dashboards and the respective principles.[33] The next section provides a detailed explanation about how the different dashboards (and the visuals within them) adhere to the principles.

Table 5.1—Overview of dashboard and its respective principles.

Cohort	Dashboard	Interactive	Purposeful	Supporting	Explanation	Proposition on Cognition
1	C	–	–	–	Poorly designed visuals (as observed in several business intelligence [BI] solutions), that is, not conscious design (or use) of visuals	Improving
2	D	–	–	++	Enhanced design (as observed in several BI software packages with attention to the specific PPM context)	
3	B	+	+++	++	Current design (contextualized BI design)	
4	A	+++	++	–	Designs from professional designers and architects, who were introduced and coached on PPM problem solutions	

Legend
+++ Principle is very salient in the visual
++ Principle is salient in the visual
+ Principle features in the visual, but to a considerably limited extent
– Principle is violated

---

[33] Further detail on the operationalization of visual design and the dashboard itself can be found in Section 5.4.1.

Participants were randomly assigned to four cohorts (1, 2, 3, and 4), each using a different dashboard to execute the same decision task. After the completion of the decision task, a random subgroup of Cohorts 1, 2, and 3 was assigned an extra decision task to be undertaken with a different dashboard (Dashboard A).

After each decision task, other dependent variables (familiarity, number of visuals used, and confidence in decision), demographics, and individual differences were assessed through a post-experimental questionnaire, so propositions could be explored. Open research questions were addressed through a post-experimental interview and questionnaire.

5.3 The Decision Task

The development of the experimental scenario, in this case the decision task, is of utmost importance to ensure validity of findings. A balance between realism and simplicity is of critical importance for a behavioral experiment (Grossklags, 2007). The scenario needs to be complex enough to avoid oversimplification and decision with clear "right" and "wrong" outcomes. Yet, it should be doable in short duration and by people with limited knowledge of project portfolio management.

We have used a project portfolio decision scenario developed and successfully applied in previous research (Arlt, 2010). The scenario was developed based on Arlt's experience with the portfolio of an existing organization. The case was anonymized and modified with the aim of balancing simplicity and realism.

The decision plays out in a software development company and is summarized as follows:

> The portfolio was limited to a manageable choice set of 16 projects. For each project, 15 attributes and metrics were provided, including long-term benefits and cost; short-term benefits, cost and resource needs; project duration; and several additional metrics, relevant to the portfolio decision. These metrics include both short- and long-term ROI, confidence of success, the degree of innovation and the degree of support articulated in committee votes. Participants were also provided with a detailed introduction to the experiment, including problem statement, context and strategy, as well as a concise overview for all projects, including project descriptions, explanation of benefits and additional, and decision-relevant information. (Arlt, 2010, p. 183)

The decision task was to choose projects for the next fiscal year, given the challenges summarized in the following bullet points and in Figure 5.1. The context, as described by Arlt (2010), was that "[a] (hypothetical) company, BMSI, is a software vendor facing [the following situation]:

- Sharp decline in earnings and significant loss in 2009, and no cash reserves;
- Competitive disadvantage due to outdated (software) product;
- Consensus-oriented culture, which means projects with only one sponsor have no chance of success;

- CEO's strategy consists of three elements: First and foremost, restore short-term financial success, second, return to developing state-of-the-art solutions and lastly, put the focus back on the customer;
- 16 candidate projects and limited financial and human resources to implement; and
- The portfolio management team interpreted and further operationalized the strategy: Achieve at least 10% increase in customer satisfaction rating and scrutinize projects without positive ROI." (p. 184)

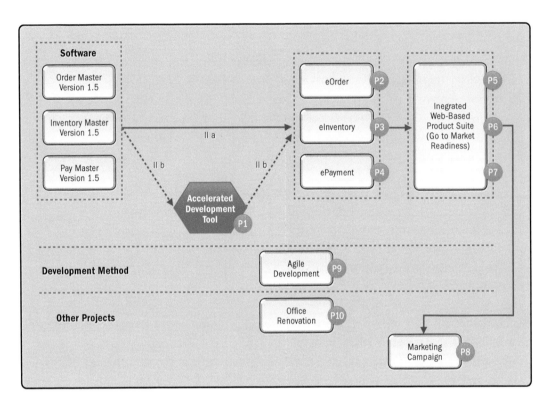

Figure 5.1—Interdependencies in a roadmap format (Arlt, 2010, p. 135).

Behind the decision task there were three potential strategic options:

- Focus on short-term revenue (choice of projects 13 and 14): This is the best solution, as it is the only one that gets close to the target short-term return.
- Focus on innovation (choice of a combination of projects 1 to 6): This led to higher innovation but compromised short-term return significantly.
- Balanced solution (choice of project 13, plus a combination of projects 1 to 6): This provided a quick fix for current software, with a reasonable short-term return, but still prepared for the long term by starting the innovation program.

5.4 Key Variables and Introduction to the Dashboards

Table 5.2 provides an overview of how the variables were operationalized. The following sections explain the operationalization in detail.

Table 5.2—Overview of the operationalization of variables.

Dependent Variable	Cognition	Decision quality	Number of mistakes (sum of logical mistakes and constraints exceeded)
			Strategic fit score (combination of resulting figure of three strategic priorities: short-term return, increase in customer satisfaction and innovation), and strategic choice (focus on short term, on innovation, or on a balanced strategy)
	Confidence in decision		Confidence in decision (from 1, very low, to 5, very high)
Independent Variables	Design	Adherence to design principles	Different dashboards (independent samples)
		• Interactive	Most salient feature of Dashboard A
		• Purposeful	Most salient feature of Dashboard B
		• Supporting principles (truthful, efficient, aesthetic)	Most salient feature of Dashboard D
		• Adherence to none of the principles	Dashboard C
	Use	Use of visuals displaying different perspectives of the portfolio problem	Number of visuals used
		Choice of visuals	Which visuals were used
	User	Visual literacy	Familiarity of visuals used
Control Variables	Confidence	Individual confidence independent from experimental task	Difference between correct answers and confidence in the answers
	Analytical thinking	Ability to understand instructions and think logically	% of correct answers in Bruine de Bruin et al.'s test[34]

5.4.1 Visual Design

Designers were engaged to develop the four different dashboards. Our first step was to familiarize the designers with the portfolio problem in general, the specific portfolio decision case used in the experiment, and the guiding principles of design. The creation process was iterative and involved the design of visuals by designers and their evaluation and discussion together with the research team and other potential users. As a critical element of the design process, the research problem and questions were explained to and discussed with the designers in several interactive sessions, in order to allow them to properly translate the decision problem into several designs. The result was Dashboards B, C, and D. Dashboard A is the product of another related research project[35] that involved architects, designers, and knowledge architects who were asked to translate the portfolio problem into their school of thinking and visual representation using their domain-specific visualization tool set.

Dashboards A, B, C, and D are displayed in the next pages. Dashboard A is interactive and therefore cannot be fully experienced in this static book. Screenshots of its different functionalities were used to provide the reader with an impression of the dashboard's functionality. In Dashboards B, C, and D, we have added squares and respective labels to identify each visual. These labels were used in the data analysis to refer to the specific visuals in each of the dashboards.

---

[34] The questions derive from the measurements on decision competence (Bruine de Bruin et al., 2007), specifically the subject's ability to understand and follow rules. This was of utmost importance in the decision scenario.

[35] The authors acknowledge the designs from the 2012 "Solve Different" project.

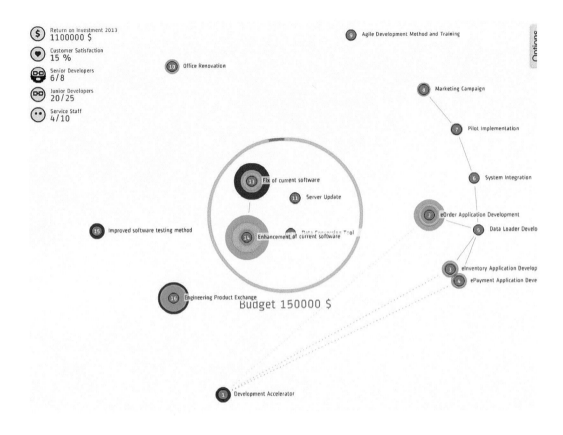

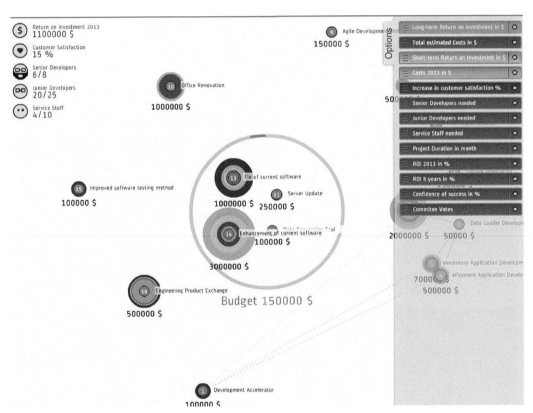

Dashboard A—Because this dashboard is interactive, we have made screenshots of its instructions and examples of its use.

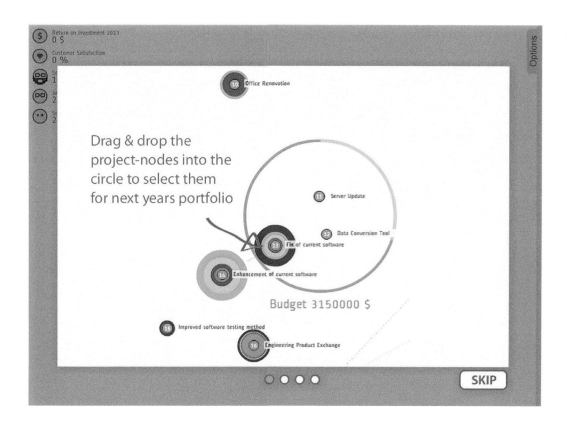

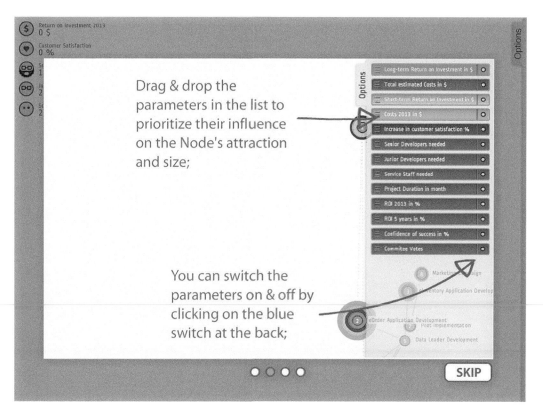

Dashboard A—*Continued.*

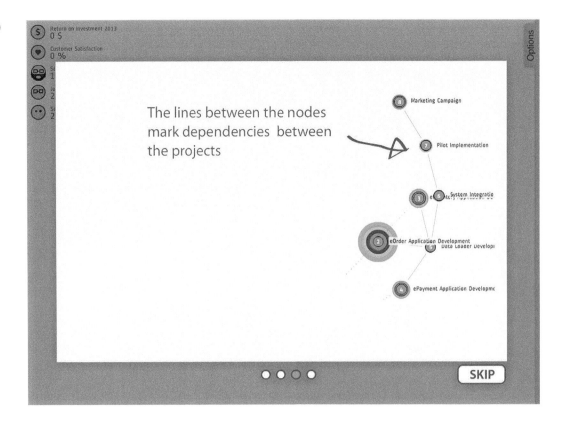

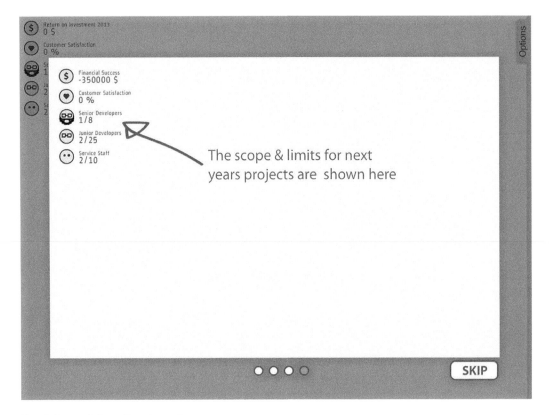

Dashboard A—*Continued.*

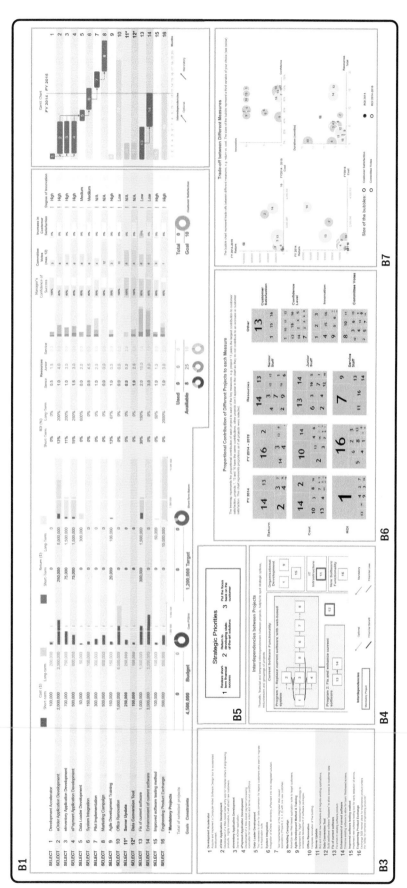

Dashboard B

VISUALS MATTER!

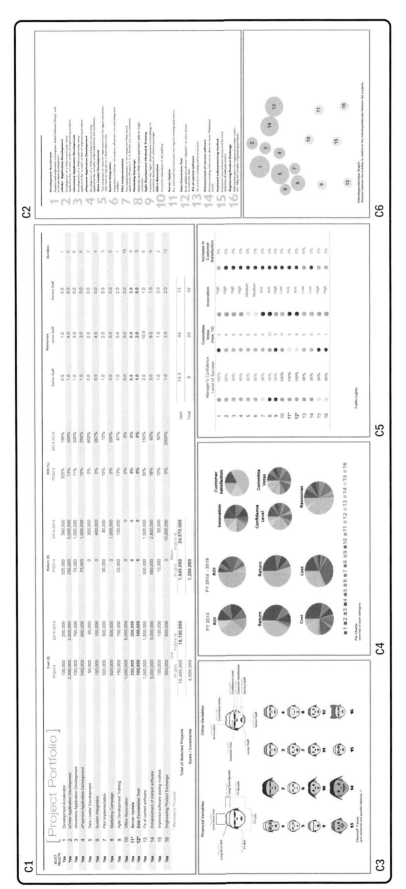

Dashboard C

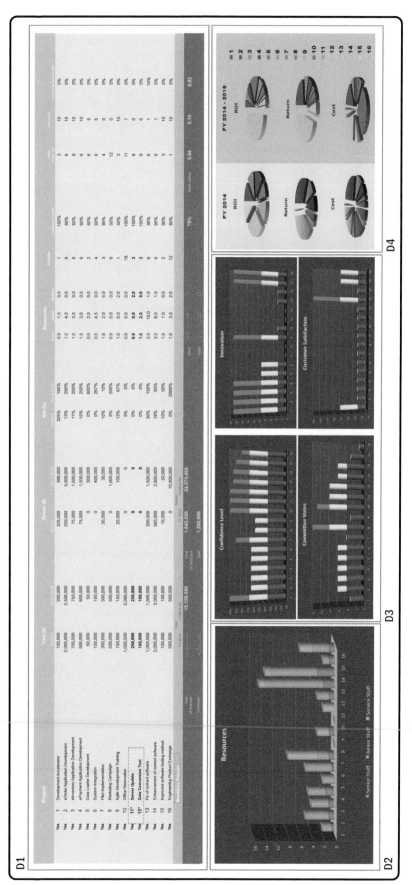

Dashboard D

VISUALS MATTER!

Dashboard	Visual	Visual Description	Adhered Principles		
			Interactive	Purposeful	Supporting
A			+++	++	0
B		Overall retrospective evaluation	+	+++	++
	B1	Table augmented with visuals	+	+++	+++
	B2	Gantt chart	–	+++	++
	B3	Short description of projects	–	+	+
	B4	Flow chart displaying thematic, financial, and temporal interdependencies between projects	–	+++	++
	B5	Reminder of strategic priorities	–	+	+
	B6	Treemap (proportional contribution of each project to each of the key decision variables)	–	+++	0
	B7	Bubble chart	+	–	–
C		Overall retrospective evaluation	–	–	–
	C1	Table	+	–	–
	C2	Short description of projects	–	+	++
	C3	Chernoff face (uses facial characteristics to represent decision variables)	–	–	–
	C4	Pie chart	–	–	–
	C5	Traffic light in table format	–	–	+
	C6	Circle proximity represents interdependencies between projects	–	+	–
D		Overall retrospective evaluation	–	–	++
	D1	Table	+	+	+
	D2	3-D bar chart displaying use of resources	–	+	+
	D3	3-D bar chart displaying random decision variables	–	–	+
	D4	3-D pie chart	–	–	–

Legend
+++ Principle is very salient in the visual
++ Principle is salient in the visual
+ Principle features in the visual, but to a considerably limited extent
– Principle is violated
0 Principle was not relevant in the visual

Table 5.3 provides a detailed description of how different visuals within each dashboard adhere to the guiding principles. As the table demonstrates, the dashboards did a reasonable job in the operationalization of the design principles. Yet, this was not a straightforward task:

- All static dashboards (B, C, and D) had one interactive visual (the table), because the task required participants to examine the impact of chosen projects on decision variables, yet they were considerably less interactive than Dashboard A.
- Visuals can have different degrees of adherence to principles, and despite our efforts, visuals within a dashboard had slightly different adherence to principles. We addressed this challenge by ensuring that the operationalized principle was the most salient characteristic of the majority of visuals within the dashboard.
- A dashboard is more than the sum of the visuals. This was particularly notable in Dashboard D. Each visual in Dashboard D does not support our principles considerably better than other dashboards. Yet, overall the

dashboard adheres to supporting principles by excelling in efficiency (see Table 5.3 for a detailed explanation).

- Supporting principles were grouped together, as they are generic design principles known to be applicable and likely to be valid in different contexts. The grouping of principles considerably reduced the required sample size and the complexity of the analysis of the results.
- In hindsight, we have identified some issues with some visuals within each dashboard, namely B7 was not as purposeful as we intended it to be, and D4 does not comport with our supporting principles. (See the detailed retrospective analysis of the dashboards and visuals in Section 6.7.)

5.4.2 Number of Visuals Used

In the post-experimental survey, participants were asked to mark all visuals that they used within their dashboard. Each participant was also asked in the interview to explain why he or she used the visuals and how. The purpose of this question was twofold. First, it helped control for participants who would choose to respond that they used all visuals, despite the fact that they didn't. Second, it provided an indication of why and how the specific visuals were used, in order to address question 2: "How do people react to different visuals?"

5.4.3 Familiarity

Familiarity was measured in a similar manner: In the post-experimental survey, participants were asked to rate their degree of familiarity with each of the visuals used in the experiment (whether from their dashboard or not). Based on these values, we calculated the familiarity of the visuals used as the average of familiarity across all visuals used.

5.4.4 Cognition

Throughout the literature review we discussed cognition in the portfolio context. Chapter 3 examined cognition under the light of information processing theories, and focused our research effort on cognition of data, that is, one's ability to engage with data mindfully to inform portfolio decisions. Through measuring decision quality, we approximate a measurement for the degree of problem understanding, as the link between cognition and decision outcomes has been already established in previous research (Ariely, 2008; Bazerman, 2009; Staw, 1981; Tversky & Kahneman, 1974). Drawing on the relationship between cognition and decision outcome is particularly acceptable in experimental settings, which neutralizes variables such as personal interests, politics, and group dynamics (e.g., Dean & Sharfman, 1996; Eisenhardt & Zbaracki, 1992). Hence, it is expected that if, for example, the participant understood the interdependencies between projects, he or she would take them into consideration when selecting a portfolio.

We investigated decision quality on two levels. On a more basic level, decision quality meant not making mistakes. Mistakes in the portfolio decision included, for example, exceeding budgetary or resource constraints, ignoring mandatory projects, or disregard for interdependencies between projects. On a more advanced level, participants could demonstrate their strategic understanding of the decision problem through improving the degree of strategic alignment between the stated objectives and their portfolio choices.

Specifically, we considered the following:

- Number of mistakes indicates a basic understanding of the problem (N = 204):
  - Number of logical mistakes (when the selected portfolio disrespected interdependencies between projects or nonselection of mandatory projects)
  - Number of constraints exceeded (when the selected portfolio exceeded budget and resource constraints)
  - Number of mistakes (total number of mistakes, calculated as a sum of the number of logical mistakes and the number of resources exceeded)
- If the participant had demonstrated a basic understanding of the problem, the strategic understanding of the problem was evaluated (N = 125):
  - Match between decision and strategic objectives

We evaluated the match between decision and strategic objective as follows. The description of the problem stated three strategic goals: short-term return (in USD), increase in customer satisfaction (in percentage value), and innovation (sum of an innovation score for each project, which ranges from 0 to 3), in this order of priority. The values for each of these three variables were normalized to a score from 0 to 1, and a strategic fit score was calculated as follows:

$$\text{Strategic fit score} = \text{Short-Term Score} * 3 + \text{Customer Satisfaction Score} * 2 + \text{Innovation Score}$$

When appropriate, we also explored participants' strategic choices (see Section 5.3).

5.4.5 Confidence in Portfolio Decision

We inquired about the participants' confidence in the decision they made during the experiment through a question in the post-experimental survey. Participants rated the statement "I am confident that I selected the projects that best benefit the company" on a Likert scale from 1 (completely disagree) to 5 (completely agree). This is a commonly used and accepted operationalization of confidence (e.g., Bruine de Bruin et al., 2007; Hall, Ariss, & Todorov, 2007; Insabato et al., 2010).

5.4.6 Control Variables

The results were controlled for analytical thinking, overall confidence of the participants, and demographics (e.g., age, education level, gender). Operationalization of demographic values is straightforward. All variables were measured through a post-experimental survey.

Overall Confidence

Overall confidence is the confidence level that participants have in their decisions—independent from the experiment. This information was gauged through a questionnaire proposed by Bruine de Bruin et al. (2007). The questionnaire involves factual questions, which each respondent rates as "true" or "false," and, for each question, the respondents are asked to rate how confident they are about this decision on a scale from 50% (just guessing) to 100% (absolutely sure). A score is created by calculating the difference between the mean percentage of confidence and the percentage of correct answers. Overconfidence refers to a higher confidence than correctness of the answer. In this case, scores would be below 100. The opposite indicates underconfidence and results in a score above 100. A score of 100 indicates a realistic assessment by the participant, as confidence and correctness of the answer match.

Analytical Thinking

Analytical thinking is likely to influence the ability of the participant to understand the portfolio problem and make superior decisions. Therefore, controlling the results for analytical thinking is important. However, the measurement of analytical thinking is not straightforward. We decided to use a reduced version of Bruine de Bruin et al. (2007) questionnaire to assess analytical thinking as the participants' ability to read and understand the problem and apply it in their decisions. This measurement was deemed appropriate because such evaluation reflected the skills necessary in the portfolio selection exercise.

The calculation from the questionnaire produced a score on a 0 to 100 scale, respective to the percentage of correct answers to the questions. Zero percentage correctness could have been caused by participants who didn't sincerely attempt to solve the problem, as the first question was straightforward and should have been answered correctly by virtually any student admitted to university. Eight people fell into this category and their analytical thinking scores were disregarded in the data analysis.

5.5 Subjects

The selection of subjects for the experiment draws on University College London's student population from a variety of disciplines. It is debatable whether student populations can be expected to behave similarly to managers—some argue in favor (Ball & Cech, 1996), while others, for example, in certain group experiments, argue against it (Potters & Van Winden, 2000). Yet students are an appropriate pool of subjects for our experiment for at least three reasons. First, the diversity of disciplines is suitable, because portfolio decisions are likewise multidisciplinary. As engagement with the visual is influenced by disciplines, it is important to ensure a diversity of disciplines to emulate portfolio decisions. Second, professionals involved in portfolio decisions are often familiar and connected to the projects and data presented to them. They also defend different interests and preferences. Such behavior impacts decisions and is difficult to emulate in experimental settings. This constitutes a challenge to our experiment, because it adds further variables and shadows the impact of visuals on decisions. The experimental setting drawing on student populations helps reduce such biases, as students are not attached to the projects to be selected, nor do they have experience in portfolio decisions.[36] Third, although students do not typically have experience in project portfolio decision making, they are expected to deal with the decision tasks appropriately, because they are used to decision problems in the context of numerous exercises during their studies.

Participation in the experiment was voluntary and anonymous. Subjects were invited to participate through an email sent to all UCL students and reminders through the UCL psychology subject pool. A random sample of 204 participants took part in the experiment. A subset of 39 participants consisted of management students who participated in the experiment as part of their classes on project portfolio management. Post-experimental analysis indicated no significant difference on decision quality and confidence between these participants and the rest of the sample.

Next to simplicity and realism is the provision of incentive, a third critical decision in the design of experiments. Reward payments to the participants were based on customary incentives at University College London; students received GBP 15 for 2 hours and had the opportunity to earn an additional performance reward of GBP 5 if they met or exceeded threshold values for expected return, innovation, and customer satisfaction. The aim of the reward was to ensure that participants would engage with the problem and try to resolve it to the best of their abilities, rather than concluding the experiment in the shortest time possible.

5.6   Location and Workflow of the Experiment

The experiment took place in a large, quiet, and closed space with a computer pool with high-resolution monitors and two sound-isolated meeting rooms. The dashboards were displayed on PCs with high-resolution

---

[36] Yet, we are aware that this choice constitutes a challenge for the generalization of the results to portfolio decisions. Future research could explore how the design of visuals would act on sensemaking, either shifting the attention from a focal point of interest, or emotional attachment to a certain project, or strengthening (according to, e.g., visual design).

displays.[37] Participants could experiment with different decision scenarios and understand their impact on different metrics (e.g., customer satisfaction, short-term return, etc.). The post-experimental survey was web-based and had been completed on the same computer as the decision. Post-experimental interviews took place in the meeting rooms.

The experiment consisted of two iterations:

1. Subjects only made one portfolio decision.
2. Subgroup of subjects had an extra task to solve with a different visual.

The experiment's workflow is summarized in Table 5.4.

Table 5.4—Experimental workflow.

Iteration		Step		Allocated Time (min)
1	**2**			
X	X	1	Hand out the instructions	1
X	X	2	Decision task	50
X	X	3	Post-experimental survey (specific questions about the decision task, demographic, and decision-making competence)	20
	X	4	Extra decision task	15
	X	5	Post-experimental survey (specific questions about the decision task)	10
X	X	6	Post-experimental Interview	10
X	X	7	Validation of completion, payment, and receipt	5

The participants were given a time limit of 45 minutes to conduct the analysis. The time used varied from around 25 minutes to one hour.

Two pilot sessions were conducted. The first pilot included two trusted people who provided detailed feedback on the experimental instructions, dashboard functionality, and overall experimental setup. The experiment was then tested with 10 subjects under the above-described conditions and recruitment process. The experiment proved stable after the second trial, as participants had no questions for clarification.

5.7   Validity and Reliability

Every research design is subject to limitations. The difficulty lies in whether the research design and the interpretation of the results correspond to what is happening in the empirical world, and whether interpretations and suggestions can be generalized back to the empirical world. Figure 5.2 displays the classic gaps in this process.

The next paragraphs evaluate how this study addressed these gaps and point to research limitations.

---

[37] We selected a lab with 27-inch 2560x1440 resolution retina displays to allow for high-quality visualization and maximum information density without the distraction of toggling or scrolling through multiple screens.

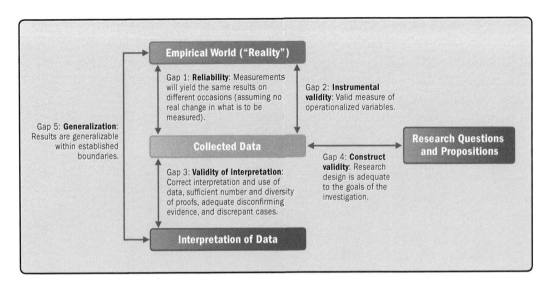

Figure 5.2—Overview of generic validity and reliability challenges (based on Geraldi, 2008).

Gap 1: Reliability

- The experiment was well designed and robust. Research instruments were standardized and based on structured interviews and questionnaires. This contributes to high levels of reliability.

Gap 2: Instrumental validity

- The careful design and reuse of tested instruments of the experimental decision tasks and questionnaire contributed to the development of valid measurements of operationalized variables.
- We have encountered an unexpected issue with the measurement of analytical thinking: Exploring the impact of visuals on people with strong analytical thinking is relevant. Professionals involved in portfolio decisions usually hold high-ranked positions in organizations and are expected to have reasonable analytical thinking. The same would be expected of students from an elite university. However, participants' scores for analytical skills were lower and more widespread than expected. Owing to the design of the experiment, the sample was stratified across different visual designs, and, in some cases, the sample of students with high scores in analytical thinking for each design became too small for statistical analysis. In such cases, qualitative analysis provided indicative findings. This issue demands a careful interpretation of the results. First, this analytical thinking test was not conducted with managers involved in portfolio decisions; hence, we cannot assume a difference in analytical thinking between the random sample of student and manager populations. Second, we need to ponder the validity of measuring analytical thinking. Not to strain participants, a limited amount of questions was used. Overseeing one aspect of a question would, therefore, have a significant and possibly

inappropriate impact on the score for analytical thinking. Given that the measurement was done through a questionnaire after the decision task, students may have been tired, and may have made mistakes. Thus, the analytical thinking score should be considered only as indicative. Third, even if the measurement for analytical thinking is valid, and some of the findings would not be applicable to highly analytical managers, the findings are still useful to inform how managers can shape visuals in communication with wider audiences.

Gap 3: Validity of interpretation

- This was ensured through a careful analysis of the data, including control for demographic variables and decision competencies, careful assessment of assumptions of different statistical methods used, and thorough and careful discussions about interpretation of the results among the research team.
- As mentioned above, the variety of the student population also increased the complexity of the data, and some propositions could only be addressed partially. In these cases, data provided indications and raised questions instead of statistically validating propositions. Larger samples would have been welcomed to cope with this variety. We have addressed this problem by conducting a very careful analysis of the results, not only drawing on complex statistical analysis but also on descriptive and qualitative analysis.
- Because participants used only a few visuals of the dashboards, propositions related to the number of visuals used could not be statistically verified, in particular Proposition 2a, which states that there is a nonlinear relationship between the number of visuals used and the cognition of data.

Gap 4: Construct validity

- Overall, we attempted to provide a transparent and logically robust explanation of propositions and operationalization of constructs and variables. Therefore, we are confident of the construct validity of the research.
- The most challenging aspect of the research design was to design dashboards that would adhere to the different design principles proposed in the research. We have engaged designers in this task, and controlled the design by portfolio expert consultation and experimental pilots. Yet, designs can adhere to principles in varying degrees and can still be perceived by each user differently. Thus, it is difficult to ensure that the dashboards provided a perfect operationalization of the design principles. We faced two problems specifically. First, all tables were partly interactive, as the participants needed to have a way to choose different projects and check their impact on the figures. Without this level of interaction, it would have been impossible to execute the experiment. We mitigated this effect by making all other visuals static, and limiting the interaction to only the choice of the

projects, which were made in a super table, present in Dashboards B, C, and D. Yet, this made the table quite powerful, and hence the most used visual in the experiment. Second, the table was also purposeful, in the sense that it displayed whether the project chosen exceeded constraints or not, a very important perspective in this decision problem.

- Our operationalization of the principle "interactive" through Dashboard A was also particularly challenging as it did not provide a visualization of the structural complexity of the problem, but instead reduced it by not allowing participants to violate constraints and interdependencies. This was intentional, as current interactive visuals (or tools) tend to do exactly that—reduce complexity. As we discussed in the data analysis (i.e., participant reactions), this led to two different decision approaches: one which opted for a mindless trial and error of different decision options, and the other, which used the visual to address questions in a process of developing a more elaborate understanding of the strategic problem.

Gap 5: Generalization (external validity)

- We aim for local generalization of the results, that is, not to all decision problems, but to portfolio contexts. As Grossklags (2007) points out, economic experimentalists aim for a more local form of external validity test called parallelism in which they evoke a more narrow relationship between small-scale experiments and realistic markets. Given the main characteristics of the economic environment observed in the field and modeled in the laboratory, they argue that observations from the experiment will then carry over into these closely related real-world institutions and can be further validated by field data (Grossklags, 2007).
- In our analysis, local generalization of results carefully considers the differences between the populations of students and managers, as discussed above.

CHAPTER 6

Data Analysis

6.1 Research Questions and Propositions

Throughout Chapters 4 and 5, propositions and questions have been proposed and discussed. These are summarized in Table 6.1 and Figure 6.1, and will be tested empirically in this chapter.

Table 6.1—Summary of research propositions and questions.

Main research question	How to use and design visuals to support cognition of data in portfolio decisions?	
	Proposition and questions	
Design	Proposition 1a:	Cognition of data is positively influenced by adherence to design principles (interactive, purposeful, and supporting).
	Proposition 1b:	Confidence is positively influenced by adherence to design principles (interactive, purposeful, and supporting).
	Proposition 1c:	Despite negative implications of change (e.g., adoption problems, learning curve), improvement of visual design positively impacts cognition of data.
Use	Proposition 2a:	There is a nonlinear relationship between the number of visuals used and the cognition of data.
	Proposition 2b:	The use of more visuals contributes to an increase in confidence and can lead to overconfidence.
User/Designer	Proposition 3a:	Cognition is positively influenced by familiarity with the visuals used.
	Proposition 3b:	Confidence is positively influenced by familiarity with the visuals used.
Relationship	Proposition 4:	There is a correlation between design, use, and user.
Questions	Question 1:	**How do people use visuals?**
	Question 2:	**How do people react to different visuals?**

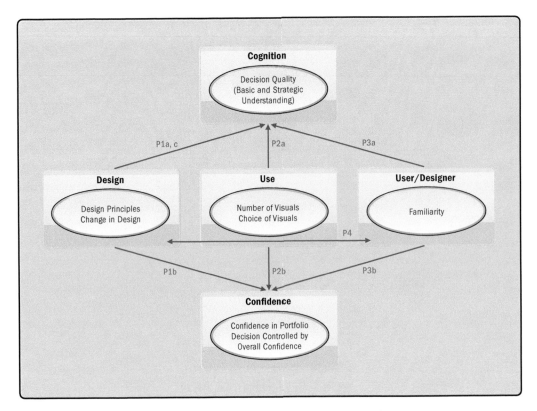

Figure 6.1—Overview of specific research propositions and questions.

6.2 Demographics

Table 6.2 provides an overview of our sample's demographics across different dashboards.

The impact of demographics and control variables on dependent variables was tested through the Mann-Whitney-U Test (gender and experience in decisions), the Kruskal-Wallis H Test (area, age, and education level), and Pearson's correlation (analytical thinking score, overall confidence score). The analysis suggests that number of mistakes should be controlled for age[38] and analytical thinking, and short-term score should be controlled for analytical thinking.[39,40] As expected, confidence in the decision should be controlled for overall confidence.[41]

---

[38] $\chi^2(3) = 20.139^{***}$ where participants who are under 25 years old have a lower number of mistakes and logical mistakes than participants age 26–35 and those who were 36–45 years old. Significant results are taken into consideration, which means that the identified relationship or correlation is more than mere random chance. The following notation indicates different significant levels throughout the research: * Significant at the 0.05; ** Significant at the 0.01; *** Significant at the 0.005.

[39] We have established a weak but significant impact of analytical thinking in numbers of mistakes $(-.205^{**})$ and with short-term scores $(.250^{**})$.

[40] It is particularly important to control for these variables, because, although we randomly assigned dashboards to participants, the sample of each dashboard is significantly different in terms of age $(\chi^2 = 22.145^{***}$, where Dashboard A had significantly younger participants than Dashboards B, C, and D) and analytical thinking $(\chi^2 = 10.594^{**}$, where Dashboards B and C had more intelligent participants than Dashboards A and D).

[41] Correlation of $-.205^{**}$ was established. It is negative because lower measurements indicate overconfidence and higher underconfidence. The confidence on decisions was measured in the opposite scale (i.e., the higher the measure, the higher their confidence).

Table 6.2—Sample's demographics.   **85**

		Total		A		B		C		D	
		Freq	%	Freq	%	Freq	%	Freq	%	Freq	%
Gender	Female	111	54%	29	59%	32	60%	24	47%	26	51%
	Male	90	44%	20	41%	20	38%	26	51%	24	47%
Age	Under 25	131	64%	44	90%	29	55%	29	57%	29	57%
	25-35	54	26%	2	4%	19	36%	16	31%	17	33%
	36-45	12	6%	3	6%	3	6%	4	8%	2	4%
	46-60	0	0%								
Education Level	High School	60	29%	33	67%	8	15%	8	16%	11	22%
	Undergraduate Degree	72	35%	12	22%	23	43%	22	43%	15	29%
	Post-graduate Degree	66	32%	4	8%	19	36%	19	37%	24	47%
	Doctorate	3	1%	0	0%	2	4%	1	2%	0	0%
Specialty	Architecture and Design	10	5%	1	2%	2	4%	5	10%	2	4%
	Biology/Medicine	30	15%	4	8%	12	23%	7	14%	7	14%
	Business	36	18%	21	43%	8	15%	2	4%	5	10%
	Education	0	0%								
	Mathematics/ Computer Science	28	14%	9	18%	5	9%	9	18%	5	10%
	Natural Sciences	11	5%	2	4%	3	6%	1	2%	5	10%
	Other	34	17%	5	10%	10	19%	8	16%	11	22%
	Social Sciences	51	25%	7	14%	12	23%	18	35%	14	28%
Experience in Decisions at Work	No	119	58%	36	74%	31	59%	30	59%	22	43%
	Yes	82	40%	13	27%	21	40%	20	39%	28	55%
Missing		3	1%	0	0%	1	2%	1	2%	1	2%

6.3 Proposition 1: Impact of Visual Design on Cognition and Confidence

This section explores Proposition 1 (the impact of visuals on the cognition of data and on confidence depends on the *design* of the visuals), and the specific propositions (1a and 1b). The next paragraphs provide further details on the analysis.

Proposition 1a: Impact of Visual Design on Cognition

Cognition was operationalized as decision quality, which in turn was assessed as number of mistakes (for basic understanding), and strategic fit score and strategic choice (for strategic understanding).

The analysis suggests a positive and significant impact of visual design on number of mistakes.[42] Analytical thinking scores moderate this relationship.

---

[42] Because data were not normally distributed, we conducted a descriptive analysis and a Kruskal-Wallis H test for the relationship between visual and number of mistakes within each of the different categories of analytical thinking and age, where sample sizes allowed. The total number of mistakes and number of logical mistakes was significantly different across dashboards ($\chi^2(3) = 16.230$*** and $\chi^2(3) = 18.492$***, respectively). Pairwise analysis suggested that A had significantly fewer mistakes and logical mistakes than C***, and A had fewer mistakes and logical mistakes than D*, and B fewer logical mistakes than C*. The expected differences between A and B, B and D, and C and D were not statistically significant. This result was further qualified when controlling for analytical thinking.

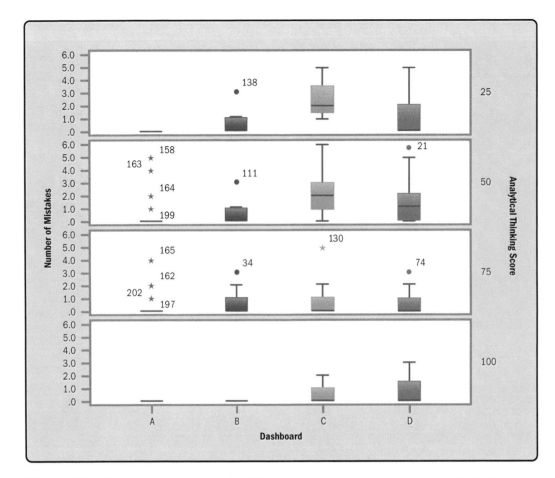

Figure 6.2—Boxplot of number of mistakes across dashboards and analytical thinking scores.

The impact of visual design on number of mistakes was not significant for high analytical thinking scores, $\chi^2(3) = 1.776$, but was significant for low and average analytical thinking scores, $\chi^2(3) = 15.756***$. A pairwise analysis of results for low and average analytical thinking scores suggests that the number of mistakes is significantly lower in Dashboard A than C*** and in B than C*. The boxplot in Figure 6.2 displays the results graphically.[43]

The results suggest that visual design did not have a significant impact on strategic fit scores.[44] Analysis of the strategic fit score indicated that only the increase in customer satisfaction score was significantly different across dashboards, $\chi^2(3) = 10.827*$, where A led to significantly higher customer satisfaction scores than C*. No significant relationship has been identified when controlling for analytical thinking.

---

[43] The impact of visuals on the number of mistakes remained similar when accounting for differences in age groups. The effect of analytical thinking scores on the relationship between visual design and number of mistakes remained across age groups.

[44] The analysis of the impact of visuals on the strategic understanding of the problem was done by comparing the differences between strategic fit score (short-term return, customer satisfaction, and innovation, and the balance between these scores) for participants using Dashboards A, B, C, and D, controlling for analytical thinking.

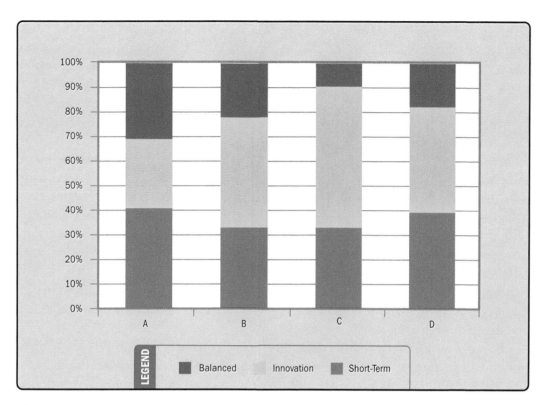

Figure 6.3—Different strategies across dashboards.

However, descriptive analysis of the strategic choice indicates some differences across dashboards. The most appropriate solution should have focused on the short-term scenario, while the second-best alternative was the innovative option. Some participants attempted to balance the two. Short-term focus was similar across different dashboards, with A and D being slightly better. However, there were fewer innovative decisions and more balanced decisions in A, followed by B and D, and then C (see Figure 6.3).

This could be because participants using Dashboard A did not clearly recognize the two potential strategic options and felt freer to try out different combinations of projects that attempted to score higher in the indicated measurements. An alternative explanation is that these participants wanted to balance different strategies, surviving at the short term, but also being in a good strategic position in the long term.

Proposition 1b: Impact of Visual Design on Confidence

The Kruskal-Wallis H Test suggests that visual design had no significant impact on confidence ($\chi^2(3) = 5.264$, p = .153).

Proposition 1c: Impact of Change on Visual Design on Cognition and Confidence

This section explores Proposition 1c, namely the impact of change in dashboard design in the experiment. Forty-four participants who first used Dashboards B,

C, or D were asked to conduct an extra task using only Dashboard A. They had 15 minutes to reevaluate their decisions based on different strategic priorities. The change in strategic priority was to balance short- and long-term return instead of focusing on short-term return only.

We chose to explore the effect of change from Dashboards B, C, or D to A for two reasons. First, Dashboard A is a very different form of seeing the problem. Dashboards B, C, and D are static visual representations, as frequently used in current portfolio dashboards, and are based on a table format supplemented with other visuals, all with detailed data about each project. Dashboard A departs from this format and molds the decision process into an intuitive tool: The participants had to drag and drop interdependent projects into a portfolio, which was displayed as a circle. The size of the circle further symbolized resource constraints. Consequently, this dashboard demands a different engagement with the problem.

Second, Dashboard A provided better support of decisions, which was confirmed empirically above (it reduced the number of mistakes significantly). Hence, we not only simulated a change to something different but also to a visual that enhanced decision quality.

We now turn to the analysis of the differences in decision quality and confidence and participants' reactions to Dashboard A after this extra task.

Descriptive analysis suggests that the decision quality of the extra task improved both in terms of mistakes[45] and strategic fit score.[46] This indicates that the use of the interactive dashboard had a positive impact on decision quality, even after a change from a static to an interactive dashboard.

Surprisingly, despite improvement in decision quality, participants were not overall more confident about their decisions. The Wilcoxon Signed Rank test indicates no significant difference in confidence between Task 1 and the Extra Task ($z = 151.0$, $p = .501$). Specifically, the results indicate that 20 participants (approximately 50%) were just as confident, 12 (approximately 30%) were more confident, and 9 (20%) were less confident. Yet, a majority of scores remained quite similar: Only one person had a much lower confidence (reducing from 4 to 2), and two improved from 2 to 4. This suggests that their confidence remained mainly the same, despite an increase in decision quality.

To cross-check this result, participants were asked to rate whether they were more or less confident about their decisions on the Extra Task in comparison with those of Task 1 and we analyzed the relationship between change in confidence and decision quality.

Figure 6.4 indicates the different decision quality changes from Task 1 to the Extra Task—what would be the expected impact on confidence—and also displays participants' respective change in confidence. Eighteen of the 44 (approximately 40%) had the expected confidence increase/decrease. Thirteen (approximately 30%) reported a decrease in confidence while having better results. This analysis reinforces the findings above that confidence was lower

---

[45] Of the 44 participants, 26 didn't make mistakes in either of the tasks; 16 others reduced the number of mistakes to 0.

[46] Fourteen improved, six maintained, and six worsened their strategic fit scores.

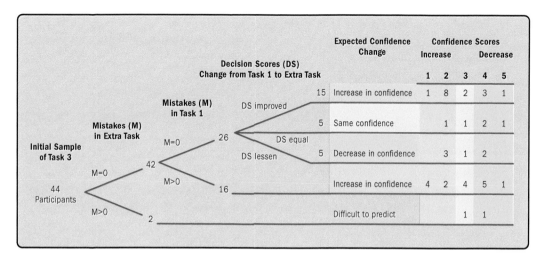

The table in the figure:

					Expected Confidence Change	Confidence Scores				
						Increase			Decrease	
						1	2	3	4	5
			15	DS improved	Increase in confidence	1	8	2	3	1
		26	5	DS equal	Same confidence		1	1	2	1
			5	DS lessen	Decrease in confidence		3	1	2	
	42	16			Increase in confidence	4	2	4	5	1
	2				Difficult to predict			1	1	

Decision Scores (DS)
Change from Task 1 to Extra Task

Mistakes (M) in Task 1

Mistakes (M) in Extra Task

M=0 26

M>0 16

Initial Sample of Task 3

M=0 42

M>0 2

44 Participants

Figure 6.4—Relationship between decision quality and confidence in the Extra Task.

than expected, and that although decision quality improved with interactive design, confidence has decreased.

Summary

In summary, the analysis suggests that visual design had an impact on cognition and confidence. Figure 6.5 summarizes the results.

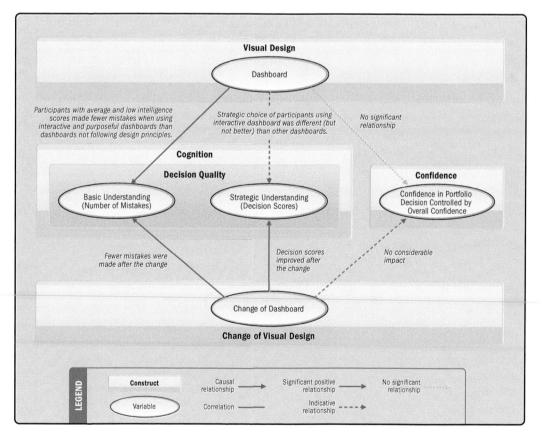

Figure 6.5—Overview of the impact of visual design on cognition and confidence.

Overall, across the tests, Dashboards A and B yield better results than D, and D better than C. This suggests that adhering to design principles leads to improved cognition, in particular, interactive and purposeful, and not adhering to principles has a detrimental effect on cognition. Yet, the influence of visuals was only significant for a basic understanding of the problem and for participants who had an average or low analytical thinking score. Therefore Proposition 1a was partly supported.

However, visual design had no significant impact on confidence, and therefore Proposition 1b was not supported.

The same pattern is also observed after a change from static to dynamic visual design. Despite negative implications of change (e.g., adoption problems, learning curve), improvement on visual design positively impacted cognition of data (i.e., it reduced mistakes and improved strategic fit). Yet, there was no significant correlation between improvement on visual design and confidence. This is intriguing. Participants improved their cognition, yet they were not necessarily more confident about it. We will discuss this in Section 6.9.

6.4 Proposition 2: Impact of Visual Use on Cognition and Confidence

The objective of the analysis was to determine the impact of the number of visuals used on participants' cognition (basic and strategic understanding) and confidence. The rationale behind this analysis is that each visual would encourage participants to take a different perspective and therefore gain a more comprehensive understanding of the problem, yet the analysis of too many visuals costs time and could lead to information overload, and potentially overconfidence (higher confidence than decision quality). The next paragraphs provide further details on the analysis.[47]

To our surprise, participants engaged with a very limited number of visuals, which limits our ability to interpret the impact of number of visuals in cognition, and hence to test Proposition 2a. Within these constraints, the data suggest that the impact of number of visuals on a basic and strategic understanding of the problem is not as strong as expected. The distribution of number of mistakes for each number of visuals used is nearly the same and no significant difference has been observed in a Kruskal-Wallis test.

Number of visuals has a weak yet significant positive correlation with confidence of .182*. Hierarchical analysis was also conducted and identified a significant yet very weak impact of number of visuals on confidence,

---

[47] Unlike Dashboards B, C, and D, Dashboard A has only one visual structure. Consequently, the sample used for this analysis was only of participants using Dashboards B, C, and D, a total of 163 observations. Four used no visuals, and only two used four visuals. These cases were considered outliers and disregarded in the analysis. The number of valid observations has, hence, reduced to 157. The Kruskal-Wallis test was used to analyze the differences between samples with more or fewer visuals.

where number of visuals explains nearly 2% variance in confidence (B = .164*, adj. R^2 = .017).[48] Therefore, Proposition 2b was supported.

Thus, the results indicate that the number of visuals had no significant impact on decision quality, but did have an impact on confidence, and led to overconfidence.

There is no significant impact of choice of specific visuals on strategic fit score or confidence,[49] but on number of mistakes, namely the use of a Gantt chart led to a significant decrease in logic mistakes (U (51) = 240.000*). This is not surprising, given that such a relationship has been already empirically established in previous research (MacNeice, 1951). Still, it supports the argument that examining different and relevant perspectives matters in portfolio decisions. Because of small sample sizes, the impact of use of other visuals could not be statistically tested.

Figure 6.6 summarizes the results of the analysis.

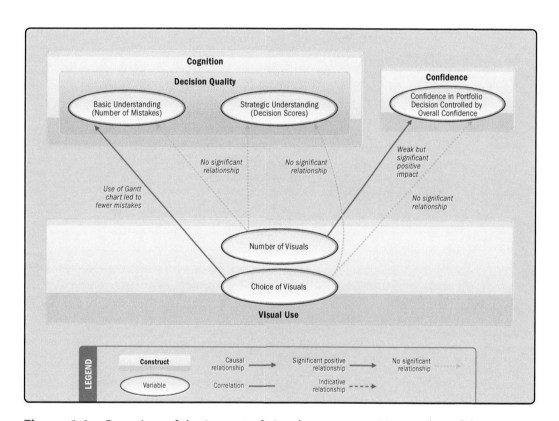

Figure 6.6—Overview of the impact of visual use on cognition and confidence.

---

[48] We conducted a hierarchical regression analysis to examine the extent to which variations in confidence could be explained by number of visuals and familiarity. The assumptions of linearity, independence of errors, homoscedasticity, unusual points, and normality of residuals were met. The results showed that number of visuals and familiarity significantly predicted around only 5% of differences in confidence. R^2 adjusted was low, of a maximum of .052** when considering both number of visuals used and their familiarity. R^2 adjusted decreased to .048** as the dashboard was included in the prediction.

[49] U(51) = 276.000, p = .307.

6.5 Proposition 3: Impact of Familiarity on Cognition of Data and Confidence

The analysis[50] does not indicate considerable impact of familiarity on cognition, as measured by number of mistakes or strategic fit score. The results also remained the same when controlling for analytical thinking scores.

Familiarity has a weak yet significant positive correlation with confidence of .232*. A hierarchical regression analysis[51] showed that number of visuals and familiarity significantly predicted around only 5% of differences in confidence.[52]

The results suggest a similar pattern to the one observed in Section 6.4. Familiarity had no significant impact on decision quality, failing to support Proposition 3a, but on confidence, supporting Proposition 3b. This indicates that familiarity can lead to a higher degree of confidence, regardless of the decision quality, as displayed in Figure 6.7.

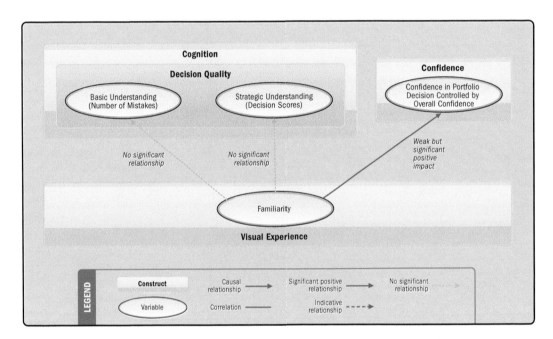

Figure 6.7—Overview of impact of familiarity on cognition and confidence.

6.6 Proposition 4: Relationship Between Visual Design, Use, and User

Our objective was to test the relationship between visual design, familiarity, and number of visuals used. In particular, we were interested to know whether the different visual designs encouraged people to engage with a larger number of visuals, and whether some visual designs were more familiar

---

[50] Due to sample size, this was explored through descriptive analysis.

[51] The assumptions of linearity, independence of errors, homoscedasticity, unusual points, and normality of residuals were met.

[52] R^2 adjusted was low, of a maximum of .052** when considering both number of visuals used and their familiarity. R^2 adjusted decreased to .048** as the dashboard was included in the prediction.

than others. In order to do so, we used descriptive statistics and conducted a Kruskal-Wallis H test.[53] Finally, we explored whether the number of visuals used and familiarity were correlated.

Number of visuals used and visual design. Dashboards B and C encouraged the engagement with a larger number of visuals than D ($\chi^2(2, 161) = 31.605***$). The reason for this seems simple. In Dashboard C, we divided the relevant data into the table and the traffic light, in order to decrease the efficiency of the visual. This means that in order to do the exercise, participants using Dashboard C had to engage with at least two visuals. These visuals, however, did not enhance the decision with an extra perspective; they were actually showing data in a very similar manner. About half of participants using Dashboard B (24 from 51[54]), by contrast, used two perspectives of the data: the table for comparisons and the Gantt chart for the schedule interdependencies between projects.

Familiarity and visual design. Data analysis shows that participants were significantly less familiar with Dashboard A compared to other dashboards ($\chi^2(3,119) = 19.001***$). This is not surprising, given that it used a completely different approach for such kinds of decisions, in an innovative design.

Although not significant, there is also an indication that participants were more familiar with Dashboard D than Dashboards B and C. This is also not surprising, as, for example, Dashboard B contains treemaps and bubble charts, which are less known than bar charts and pie charts, at least to the student population.

Figure 6.8 shows the average familiarity of the participants, not only with the visuals used but all visuals for each of the dashboards. Visuals within Dashboard B were, on average, less familiar than those in Dashboards C and D, in particular B4 (display of qualitative and financial interdependencies between projects as a block diagram), B6 (treemap), and B7 (bubble chart). Dashboard C contains Chernoff faces (C3)[55], which is a lesser-known type of visual (average familiarity 1.8). Dashboard D, in contrast, contained only well-known visuals (i.e., bar charts and pie charts and a table).

Familiarity and number of visuals used. The rationale behind this analysis is that if one is familiar with a certain visual, then he or she will be more likely to use it. Thus, our objective was to test whether visuals that were more familiar were also more likely to be used.

Descriptive analysis suggests that many visuals, which were not used, also scored low in familiarity. For example, as Table 6.3 shows, Chernoff faces, treemaps, bubble charts, and qualitative relationships were the ones that scored lowest in familiarity, and all of them have not been used frequently. Yet, although this suggests that familiarity may have influenced participants to decide whether to use a visual or not, it alone does not explain the low use of visuals of, for example, Dashboard D. Pie charts and bar charts were very familiar, yet not

---

[53] Data from Dashboard A were not considered in the analysis of the number of visuals used, because Dashboard A had only one visual, which makes the analysis pointless.

[54] Detailed analysis of the visuals used per dashboard can be found in Section 6.6.

[55] Chernoff faces use facial characteristics to represent decision variables; see the example in Dashboard C, in Section 5.4.1.

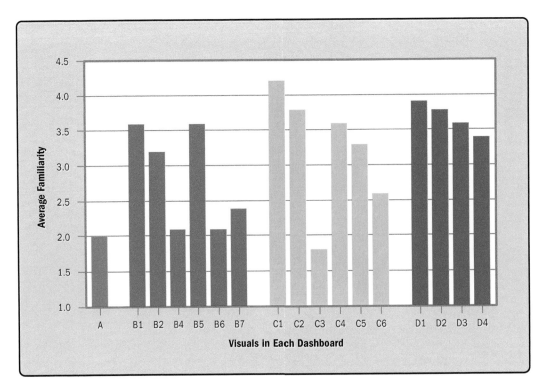

Figure 6.8—Average familiarity of different visuals.

Table 6.3—Frequency of use and familiarity of visuals.

	Visual	Frequency of Use	Familiarity		
			Mean	Standard Deviation	Valid N
B1	*Table*	50	3.6	1.4	120
B2	*Gantt chart*	24	3.2	1.4	120
B4	Qualitative relationships	4	2.1	1.1	120
B5	Strategic objective	6	3.6	1.3	120
B6	Treemap	6	2.1	1.1	120
B7	Bubble charts	2	2.4	1.1	120
C1	*Table*	48	4.2	1	120
C2	Project description	8	3.8	1.1	120
C3	Chernoff faces	1	1.8	1.2	120
C4	Pie chart	6	3.6	1.1	120
C5	*Traffic light*	24	3.3	1.2	120
C6	Interdependencies (by proximity)	4	2.6	1.3	120
D1	*Table*	48	3.9	1.1	120
D2	Bar chart resource use	4	3.8	1.2	120
D3	Bar chart	4	3.6	1.2	120
D4	Pie chart	1	3.4	1.2	120

used more frequently. We will explore further reasons for the low use of visuals in Section 6.8, which explains participants' visual preferences.

Figure 6.9 summarizes the results of the above analyses.

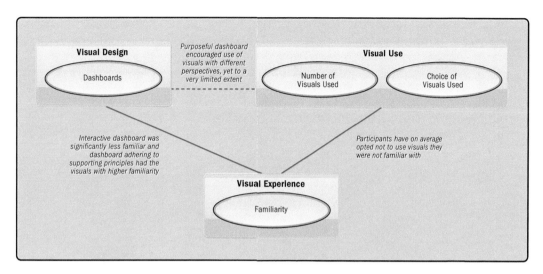

Figure 6.9—Overview of the relationship between visual design, number of visuals used, and familiarity.

6.7 How Do Different Users React to Different Visuals? Exploring Visual Preferences and Adoption

This section describes the preference for dashboards and visuals within dashboards. We first analyze dashboard preference and then look specifically into the preferences and use of specific visuals. Finally, we explore reasons for those choices.

6.7.1 Preferred Dashboard

In order to evaluate dashboard preferences, we showed participants dashboards and asked them to choose which dashboard or combination of them they would have preferred if they were to repeat the experiment. This was done in two steps:

- Step 1: We first asked participants to choose among the three static dashboards, namely Dashboards B, C, and D, or a combination of visuals from these different dashboards.
- Step 2: Thereafter, participants who used Dashboard A were asked to choose between either A or their previously preferred dashboard or both.[56]

The results from the first step suggest that around 40% of participants preferred Dashboard B over C and D. A combination between dashboards was the

---

[56] Forty-seven participants used only Dashboard A, and 43 participants used first Dashboard B, C, or D, and then Dashboard A for the Extra Task (see methodology).

second most popular option (approximately 30%), followed by D (23%), and C (8%). This confirms our expectations, as Dashboard B was designed to be better than D, which in turn was better than Dashboard C.

As displayed in Figure 6.10, the data also suggest the importance of familiarity with the dashboards. Interestingly, the percentage of participants who preferred the originally assigned dashboards over proposed alternatives is larger than the average preference for the respective dashboard. For example, only 8% of all participants chose Dashboard C, yet approximately 16% of participants who used Dashboard C preferred to keep it if they had to repeat the experiment. The same can be observed also for Dashboards B and D.

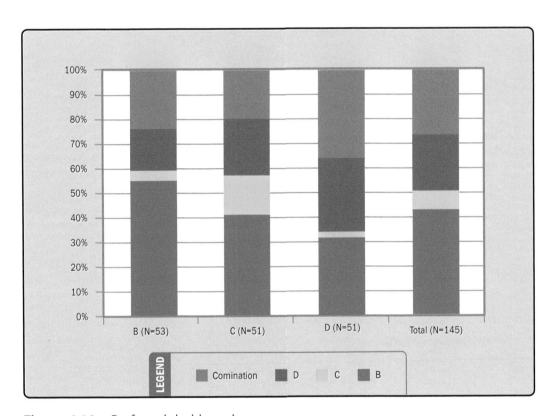

Figure 6.10—Preferred dashboards.

Figure 6.11 displays the results for Step 2, where participants were asked to choose between the preferred dashboard in Step 1 or Dashboard A. Dashboard A was conspicuously preferred over other dashboards by those participants who had already used Dashboard A (over 70% preferred Dashboard A, around 20% wished to have both Dashboard A and the preferred Dashboard from Step 1, and a minority of 5% preferred static dashboards). Yet, the preference for Dashboard A decreased significantly for those participants who first used Dashboards B, C, or D. In their case, around a third of participants chose Dashboard A, another third preferred to keep the static dashboard, and the final third opted for having both.

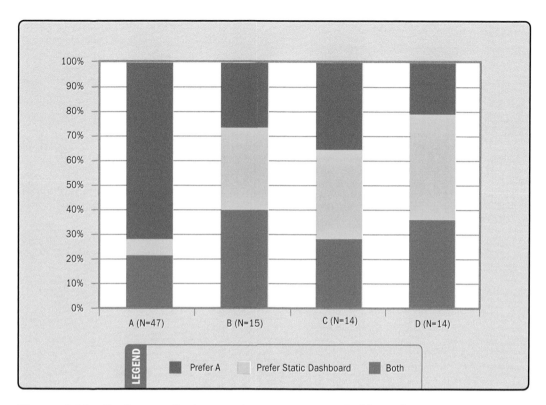

Figure 6.11—Preference for interactive versus static dashboards.

The results reinforce the importance of familiarity identified in the previous analysis. Six out of 49 participants using Dashboard A opted not to engage with the visual and made decisions based on qualitative data on projects. In the post-experimental interviews, participants reported that they didn't understand how it should work and opted for the qualitative information provided on paper. These participants had obviously made mistakes, as they did not have information on Return on Investment, innovation scores, and so forth, and hence could not make an informed decision. This explains a great majority of the mistakes made by people using Dashboard A. It also strengthens the importance of visual acceptance and familiarity.

Yet, if used, the preference for the Dashboard A is strikingly stronger than for the other dashboards. Participants using Dashboard C were more willing to change their preference. Only about 15% of the participants using Dashboard C wished to keep it, and around 35% preferred Dashboard A instead of their previously preferred static dashboard. The results suggest that these participants were looking for better options. Such behavior is less present in participants who used Dashboard D, and even less for Dashboard B. In this regard, the results indicate that resistance to change in the use of visuals appears to be related to the extent to which dashboards adhere to our principles.

6.7.2 Used and Preferred Visuals

Nearly all participants used the table displayed on the top of Dashboards B, C, and D. This suggests that participants opted for the visual that was mostly familiar, densely packed with all the relevant information, sort of interactive, and the easiest to use.[57]

When choosing a combination of visuals, participants were less reluctant to change (see overview in Table 6.4). The visuals from Dashboard B were chosen more often than others. For example, the majority of people who chose a combination of dashboards preferred a table augmented by visuals (Table B1) over tables with only numbers (Tables C1 and D1). This reinforces our previous argument that inferior visuals are more likely to be exchanged, reducing the effect of familiarity on preferences.

Participants also realized the importance of the interdependencies between projects to make portfolio decisions. The Gantt chart was the second most used visual[58] and the most frequently chosen visual, with 27 votes. The qualitative overview of the relationship between projects (B4) was also one of the most often chosen visuals (chosen 23 times).

Interestingly, there appears to be no clear relationship between the frequency of use of a certain visual and the frequency with which this visual is chosen to be

Table 6.4—Use and preference of visuals.

Code	Description	Frequency that the visual was used	Frequency that the visual was chosen for an "ideal" dashboard
B2	*Gantt chart*	24	27
B1	*Table*	50	23
B4	Qualitative relationships	4	21
D3	Bar chart	4	20
B6	Treemap	6	16
B3/C2	Project description	13	16
B5	Strategic objective	6	15
D1	*Table*	48	14
D2	Bar chart resource use	4	13
C5	*Traffic light*	24	12
B7	Bubble charts	2	12
D4	Pie chart	1	11
C4	Pie chart	6	8
C3	Chernoff faces	1	8
C6	Interdependencies (by proximity)	4	7
C1	*Table*	48	5

---

[57] Because nearly everyone used it, we could not assess the difference between using the table and not using it. The differences between using the table in Dashboard B, C, or D are analogous to the differences between the dashboards themselves, as a majority of the participants used only one visual (the table).

[58] Nineteen participants used it, approximately 36% of the participants who were offered the possibility.

part of a participant's dashboard of choice (see Table 6.4). For example, only six people used a treemap, yet 16 participants chose it after reading and evaluating all the visuals used in the experiment. Similarly, four people used the visual displaying the qualitative relationship between projects, yet 23 chose it as part of their dashboard of choice. A potential explanation for the difference between visuals used in the experiment and those chosen thereafter is that in the survey and interview, participants had more time to understand different visuals and their potential utility to the decision problem, retrospectively.

The result indicates that unlike in their preferences for dashboard, participants were quite willing to add less familiar visuals to their familiar ones. As shown in Figure 6.12, only one person chose to use the table exclusively. The majority selected between four and eight visuals for their dashboard of choice.

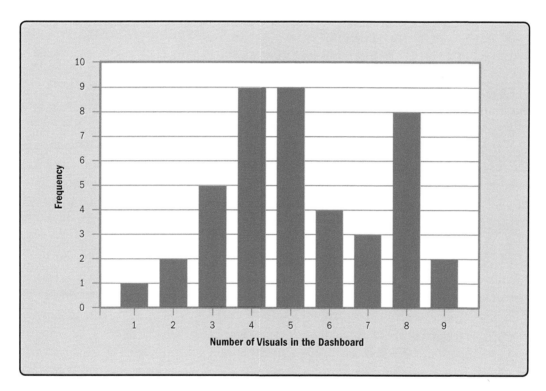

Figure 6.12—Number of visuals in participants' "ideal" dashboard.

6.7.3 Explaining Participants' Visual Preferences

Finally, we explored why participants chose certain dashboards and visuals over others through qualitative data from open questions in the questionnaire and interviews. In particular, we were interested in understanding why visuals were important and appreciated, but also used less than expected. We identified five complementary explanations for the low usage of visuals.

First, participants, regardless of the assigned dashboards, chose to use visuals they considered easy to understand, comprehensive, and quick to interpret. Participants also liked tables because they provided a comprehensive display of relevant data for the decision. Moreover, participants had to analyze the data and make decisions within a fixed time frame of 45 minutes. Under pressure, quick interpretation of the visual was paramount in the choice of which visuals were used. Visuals that appeared confusing and time consuming (mostly because they were novel to the participant) were avoided. Several participants also avoided additional visuals in order to stay focused on what they considered most relevant for the decision and to avoid information overload.

This led participants to rely mainly on tables, traffic lights, and Gantt charts (apart from the interactive Dashboard A).[59] Visuals that are tailored for comparisons of a large number of observations such as treemaps (which was key for this task) were not used, as several participants did not understand the visual at first glance.

Hence, efficiency of a visual from the perspective of a participant is not only evaluated as information density, but also as a function of speed to meaningfully interpret a visual, retrieve data, and gain insight.[60]

Moreover, participants preferred exact figures and numbers. Aggregated figures in charts were mistrusted or found less useful. This is also counterintuitive because we would expect participants to appreciate not only detailed figures, but also the need for understanding patterns and comparisons. However, some participants did so.

Second, interactive features had a striking influence on adoption. The table was the only interactive element in Dashboards B, C, and D. This is problematic because participants wanted to "see" what happens when certain choices were made. It is not surprising that interaction was important. We discussed this in our generic principles in Chapter 4, where we explained how interactive visuals constitute a paradigm shift in data visualization thinking. Yet, we did not expect it to be so relevant, as the tables were only partly interactive.[61] In hindsight, we should have made the other visuals as interactive as the table.

Third, our dashboards were not designed to improve cognition but to represent different guiding principles that we wanted to validate (see Section 5.4.1). The participants recognized the differences and showed an intuitive visual literacy. They were quite critical toward visuals and were right to be so!

For example, participants found Chernoff faces confusing and not helpful. Chernoff faces represent each variable as a feature of our face, for example, face width representing short-term costs. It draws on the fact that we can recognize small differences between human faces quickly and intuitively, and hence can easily see which projects have, for instance, wider or narrower faces. Although Chernoff faces could be useful visuals to identify distinguishing features of

---

[59] It did not encourage participants to engage with common visuals such as pie charts or bar charts. This is understandable, because the pie charts and bar charts used in Dashboards C and D were consciously designed to be less purposeful.

[60] One could argue that this effect is likely to be stronger in this experiment than in real-life situations. The experiment was "time constraint" and students are good at testing and will attempt to get through the entire test, even if cutting corners is required. Yet, managers also live under very high time pressure; hence, speed is likely to be just as relevant.

[61] See Section 5.4.1 for a detailed explanation of our need to compromise and add an element that allowed some interaction.

projects in a portfolio, the features need to be chosen very carefully, so that, for **101** example, the most attractive projects also look attractive, and the most important variables are the most visibly recognizable. The design of Chernoff faces in Dashboard C did not adhere to this, and hence ended up being neither purposeful, nor truthful, nor efficient in our decision context. The visual was confusing and would call the participants' attention to less important variables, such as committee votes.

In contrast, participants using Dashboard B often explained how they navigated from visual to visual to capture different perspectives of the problem:

> Visual 1 provides the vital information that I require to ensure that my objectives are achieved while ensuring that the constraints are met. Visual 2 and 4 provide information about the timeline of the projects, which allowed me to understand that projects 1–8 and projects 13–14 are the two main projects that cannot be completed simultaneously. Decision must be made between these two "main" projects. Visual 5 continuously reminded me of the objectives that I have to fulfill.

In summary, our proposed guiding principles were confirmed not only through quantitative data but also through qualitative analysis. Our findings also suggest that some participants had an intuitive visual literacy and were able to capture visuals that were less useful (not following principles, or not purposeful), as well as understanding the purpose of some of the visuals.

Fourth, personal preference also played an important role. Some visuals were very intuitive and helpful for some, and indigestible for others. Table 6.5 presents some extracts of contradicting opinions about the visuals in each dashboard.

Table 6.5—Indications of personal preferences.

Dashboard	Indicative Quote
A	• "The visuals used in the exercise are simpler to understand."
	• "Circles represent different volumes, distort the data. Numbers obscured by the 'option' tab. Dashboard enables 'sorting' in top to bottom order."
B	• "Visual 2 graphically aided with the constraints while Visual 4 offered an easy understanding of targets met."
	• "Visual 2 didn't display much useful information—I had already eliminated most of the projects that start later on. Visual 4: had already familiarized myself sufficiently with project interdependencies."
C	• "Pie charts are also interesting, as they give me complex data in a simple nutshell."
	• "Visual 6 provides the relations between projects, which is helpful to help us group the provided projects in a short time."
	• "Six [interdependencies by proximity] barely an effect, but the numbers and traffic lights were helpful."
D	• "Visual 1 [table] is presented at the top and the numbers are easier to read in detail. Visual 3 [bar chart with different variables] gives good overall view."
	• "I found the colors distracting and confusing." (Bar charts and pie charts)

Personal preferences may indicate varying degrees of visual literacy or they can be rooted in people's idiosyncratic experiences with visuals, mostly colored by their profession and personal interests. For example, an engineer is likely to be more comfortable with flow diagrams than an accountant.

Some participants also displayed an emotional response to their engagement with visuals, using adjectives such as *fun, unprofessional, not trustworthy* (Dashboard A), *weird, scary, distracting,* and *creepy!* (Dashboard C, Chernoff faces).

This is an important point. The management of projects and project portfolios draws on the integration of different backgrounds and will be facing heterogeneous degrees and types of visual literacy. Though our principles attempt to identify common denominators, different preferences are unavoidable and need to be accommodated in the design of visuals and communication through them.

Finally, few participants were able to phase their decision process and use visuals accordingly. This small group first attempted to familiarize themselves with the data and obtain an initial understanding of the problem. High-level comparisons, interdependencies, and strategic options were more important to them than exact figures. They also moved to the detail scrutiny of the data, and fine-tuned choices. They engaged with different perspectives of the problem sequentially and not simultaneously. By doing so, they avoided information overload.

6.7.4 Participants' Reactions to a Change from Static to Interactive Visuals

Participants were asked to rate whether their confidence had improved or decreased, and then explain why this was so.

The explanations of less and more confident participants were mostly contradicting. While some felt it was easier to do the task with Dashboard A, others felt it was more difficult; while some felt they could understand the problem better, others felt the opposite. Some appreciated that they didn't have to consider constraints and interdependencies and could therefore focus on strategic alignment; others felt that the lack of control over the calculations disempowered them and made them less able to understand and justify decisions. This strengthens the importance of personal preference, as discussed in Section 6.7.3.

The results also suggest three different approaches to Dashboard A. The first was to use the fact that the detailed calculations had been done for them and focus on a more strategic understanding of the problem. The second preferred not to adopt the tool, as they missed the detailed information and found it relevant to understand the problem holistically, and hence to be able to make better strategic choices (and justify them). A third was satisfied with just doing the decisions, and not making mistakes; they didn't appear to have used the tool to understand the problem. These different approaches point not only to different cognitive styles but also to different skills in using visuals effectively. In this respect, the different approaches confirm the importance of visual skills.

Across the analysis, we have noticed that some participants were better skilled in using visuals than others. This section summarizes the four visual skills we have identified: pick relevant and appropriate visuals, understand why they are relevant and appropriate, know how to use them, and use visuals at the appropriate moment in the sensemaking process.

Few participants were able to evaluate visuals and rapidly decide whether or not to engage with them and when to do so. Behind this are four basic visual skills. First, they look at visuals to see different perspectives, different insights into the data. They will probably be asking themselves questions such as: How can this visual help me solve this problem or make this decision? How quickly can I extract interesting insights from it? How can I use this visual in an effective matter? In other words, participants noticed how the visuals could help them solve the problem and choose *what* visuals to use, understand *why* to use them, and decide *how* to "read" them. Another interesting skill was to time the use of different visuals, that is, the participant's ability to understand *when* to use each type of visual. Given our limited cognition, learning to choose where to spend "brain energy" is important in solving complex problems.

Apart from these basic skills, we have identified advanced visual skills. These were related to the participants' visual repertoire and ability to engage effectively with unfamiliar visuals.

Visual repertoire is understood as familiarity with diverse types of visuals. The logic behind this skill is that if different types of visuals are more apt to display a certain perspective of a problem, then the higher the diversity of familiar visuals, the more one can see different perspectives of a problem. This suggests the importance of being familiar with visuals in order to capture the perspective they entail.[62]

Yet, visual skills are related not only to increasing what we know but also to being able to use previously unknown visuals effectively. This constitutes a critical visual skill, and quite a relevant one for project and portfolio managers. Such skill enables a person to navigate across different knowledge areas, and hence, helps in their integration, which is paramount for the management of projects and portfolios.

Figure 6.13 displays these skills visually.

6.9 Summary, Discussion, and Implications of Key Findings

Figure 6.14 provides a summary of the findings. The figure displays the relationships between constructs and variables that could be established in quantitative and qualitative data analysis. The relationships represented correlations (not implying causality), or causal relationships. The nature of the relationship

---

[62] Intriguingly, Section 6.5 has shown that familiarity with the visuals used had no significant relationship with the number of mistakes or strategic fit scores but only with confidence. This result suggests that familiarity increased comfort or even trust in one's own interpretation, but not necessarily decision quality. This result is counterintuitive, but can be explained by the fact that Dashboard A and B (with a better design) also scored lower in familiarity (see Figure 6.9).

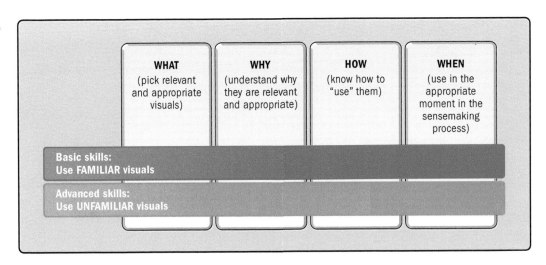

Figure 6.13—Visual literacy identified in the participants of the experiment.

identified is explained in text either in the arrow or summary of the relationship by each construct. We also specify whether there was a significant, indicative (when the relationship was only supported by descriptive analysis or sample size allowed only an indicative analysis), or no significant relationships.

The next sections summarize and discuss four key findings and propose implications for research and practice.

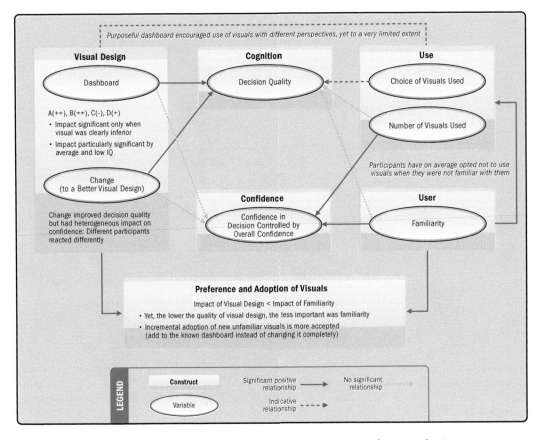

Figure 6.14—Overview of the findings of the quantitative data analysis.

First, our results support the relevance of the proposed design principles.[63] Participants with low and average analytical thinking scores made significantly fewer mistakes with Dashboard A and B than with Dashboard D. Dashboard C led to inferior decisions. This suggests that interactive and purposeful dashboards lead to more consistent results across heterogeneous decision-making teams, and hence Proposition 1a was partly supported. The number of mistakes decreased significantly with the change from static to interactive dashboards, regardless of analytical skills, supporting Proposition 1c. Thus, overall the data suggest that **adhering to design principles leads to improved cognition, in particular interactive and purposeful principles**.

The analysis also suggests that using purposeful visuals improves cognition (specifically, the use of Gantt charts reduced the number of mistakes). This is not surprising; such a relationship has already been empirically established in previous research (MacNeice, 1951). Yet it supports the argument that examining different and relevant perspectives matters in portfolio decisions. Therefore, providing or guiding decision makers to the well-designed visual impacts cognition; hence, **facilitating access to the well-designed visuals on a dashboard or in a report is helpful**.

Principles also had an effect on which visuals are adopted and preferred. Among static dashboards, Dashboard B (designed to be purposeful) was preferred over other dashboards and was perceived to provide better visual support. Dashboard A (designed to be interactive) was strikingly popular, particularly among those participants who were only confronted with this dashboard (70% of them preferred Dashboard A over others). This suggests that participants preferred dashboards that followed design principles, in particular those that were purposeful and interactive. Thus, **adherence to design principles can increase adoption of visuals**.

In conclusion, this emphasizes that good visual design for dashboards and decision tools is relevant. It also suggests that the importance and acceptance of interactive decision tools will continue to increase. However, the positive echo for Dashboard B also shows that a well-designed, purposeful visual, even if it is not interactive, will resonate with decision makers.

"Right" but Not Necessarily Confident

The experimental results suggest that there is a significant impact of visual design on decision quality but not on confidence. The same pattern was observed when changing from static to interactive dashboards: Though the decision quality improved significantly, confidence was not affected. The above pattern is still significant after controlling for participants' overall decision confidence.[64] What is counterintuitive about this result is that some participants used better-designed visuals and made better decisions, but were not more

---

[63] In technical terms, it fails to falsify Proposition 1, 1a, and 1b.

[64] Overall confidence is the confidence level that participants have in their decisions—independent from the experiment (i.e., whether they tend to be over- or underconfident).

confident about their decisions, and other participants used worse-designed visuals and made worse decisions, but were confident.

A potential explanation for the findings is that some participants made the right decisions by chance, and not because they understood the problem. This may explain the results of some participants using Dashboard A. Dashboard A is interactive and reduces the structural complexity of the problem dramatically. The visual does not allow portfolio decisions that disrespect interdependencies between projects, resource, and budget constraints. Moreover, numbers can be retrieved, but they are not a salient feature of the visual. Hence, participants can make correct decisions regardless of their understanding. Indeed, qualitative data suggest that only a few participants appreciated the reduced complexity and used Dashboard A playfully but also thoughtfully to facilitate and improve decisions and focus on a more strategic understanding of the problem.

Several participants were satisfied with just doing the decisions, and not making mistakes; they don't appear to have used the tool to understand the problem. Instead, participants intuitively "played" with the visual, and made decisions by trial and error. It is reasonable to suggest that these participants would have better results, but not necessarily higher confidence, because they did not truly understand what they were doing.

However, this explanation does not provide a full account of the findings. A potential alternative and complementary explanation is that participants had low awareness of how visuals help (or hinder) decisions. This means that, for example, participants may have used the visuals correctly, but did not trust what they were seeing. For example, they understood the relationships through a Gantt chart and hence avoided logical mistakes, but were not absolutely sure that the Gantt chart displayed all interdependencies. Likewise, some participants preferred static dashboards with detailed information about projects, as they missed the detailed information to make better strategic choices and justify them. This lack of trust may have negatively influenced confidence.

Mistrust in visuals can be positive and can indicate high levels of visual literacy. Visuals are persuasion mechanisms, never neutral, and hence they should be received with a healthy degree of mistrust, and deserve critical scrutiny—for instance, what data have been filtered out? Which perspectives does the visual show and which ones does it not show? What does the author of the visuals want to say? What are his or her interests? and so forth. Yet, bare mistrust without critical engagement would suggest (irrational) resistance to visuals. In this case, improvement in visual literacy would be beneficial. In this specific experimental setting, mistrust in purposeful visuals such as the Gantt chart suggests the need to improve visual literacy.

This has implications in practice. Portfolio decisions are, to a large extent, a reflective process. Although this is difficult to emulate in a 45-minute experiment, in reality, interacting with data, observing the consequences of choices, reflecting on choices and trade-offs, and thereby increasing confidence over time is important for the decision-making process. Thus, unlike in an experiment, when new visuals are introduced, it is important to make decision makers comfortable with their use, so they can achieve the intended objective (i.e., looking at data from different perspectives).

In contrast to the results regarding visual design, familiarity and number of visuals used significantly impact confidence, but not decision quality (i.e., they can lead to a higher degree of confidence), regardless of whether the decision quality has improved.

We expected that participants would be able to use familiar visuals well, and therefore improve their understanding of data and hence decision quality (Proposition 3a). Yet, the findings provide very weak support for this proposition. The findings, rather, suggest that familiarity increases the comfort level and acceptance, even leading to higher confidence levels, supporting Proposition 3b.

Because participants used a limited number of visuals, we could not fully explore the nonlinear relationship between number of visuals and decision quality postulated in Proposition 2a. Overall, the results indicate that the number of visuals had no significant impact on decision quality, but it did have an impact on confidence, and led to overconfidence. Yet, use of specific visuals can have a positive impact on decision quality; the results suggest that the use of Gantt charts reduced the number of mistakes significantly. The results, therefore, provide some support for the argument that the use of more visuals is not necessarily advantageous, but examining relevant perspectives matters in portfolio decisions.

As mentioned above, portfolio decision making involves a reflective process, which takes more time than what we could simulate in an experiment. Practitioners can learn to engage with several relevant visuals at different points in time, avoiding information overload. Looking for purposeful visuals is a useful guide to decide which visuals to analyze and use when communicating results to others.

Increasing Adoption of Visuals

Contrary to what we expected, participants did not engage with several visuals, not even when the visuals were purposeful (i.e., they provided relevant perspectives of the decision problem). The data suggest several reasons for such low adoption and also point to some clues to improve the adoption of visuals. These are summarized below.

1. Adherence to design principles increases the use of visuals. We intentionally developed dashboards with different qualities, and some were by design worse than others. The participants recognized these differences in quality.

2. Participants opted for easy, comprehensive, relevant, precise, and interactive visuals. Most critical—in terms of efficiency—was not the use of space but the time required to interpret a visual. This aspect cannot be stressed enough. Efficiency and "speed to make an informed decision" are critical to informed decisions.

3. When asked to choose an "ideal dashboard," participants are quite willing to add less familiar and less used visuals to their familiar ones. This suggests that incremental changes are more accepted than a radical switch

from one dashboard to another. Though this is widely recognized in the change management literature, the results indicate that it is also valid when applied to visuals.

Intriguingly, the number of visuals chosen for a preferred dashboard was considerably higher than the number of visuals actually used in the experiment. Because duration of the task was significantly correlated with the number of visuals used (Pearson correlation of .214**), one potential explanation is that participants had more time to consider different visuals after the experiment.

Another complementary and likely explanation is that participants may have added "nice to have" visuals, regardless of their actual intent to use them. This behavior is not uncommon and in fact is irrational, as explained by behavioral scientists: What appears to be a "free" option is, in fact, not free at all (Ariely, 2008). As discussed in Chapter 4, more visuals do not necessarily lead to higher cognition and will actually lead to an "added cost" of "processing time" for understanding the visuals and to potential information overload, and potentially also overconfidence. Furthermore, people may make flawed choices when "free" options are available (Ariely, 2008). If we had "charged" for additional visuals, it is very likely that participants would have composed the dashboard differently. Further research could examine such impacts.

Thus, generally, people like choices of visuals. More visuals could, however, distract decision makers, especially if decisions are being made by a team (e.g., a portfolio board), and a person refers to visuals that are unfamiliar to others. Building consensus around a limited set of visual tools may be beneficial for both cognition and communication.

4. Participants focused on what was required, not what could help. While most visuals were merely nice to have, the tables were required to make decisions. Moreover, they were somewhat interactive, as participants could immediately see the impact of their decisions. This strengthened the bias toward using tables over visuals during our experiment.

Also, the decision task used in the experiment was—at least in some sense—not complex enough. Certain visuals that would have been very effective, or even critical in larger and more complex portfolios, were nice to have in our context (i.e., they were actually not required to make decisions). Thus, visuals may be not as appreciated in contexts in which they are beneficial yet are not required. Further research could explore what would have happened if we had a more complex decision task, one with a hundred or more projects, where lists are ineffective and other visuals become critical.

In practice, portfolios in many companies are large, and hence the contribution of visuals becomes more evident. It is worth noting that users may only use visuals when required. In this respect, if a company's dashboard offers interactive tables and static visuals, one may observe a diminished engagement with the visuals, despite their potential relevance to inform the detailed choices to be made in the table. Making visuals interactive could also help overcome this

5. Familiarity is critical. Familiarity has a strong influence on the preferred dashboards. The percentage of participants who preferred the originally assigned dashboards over proposed alternatives is larger than the average preference for the respective dashboard. For example, only 8% of all participants chose Dashboard C, yet approximately 16% of participants who used Dashboard C preferred to keep it if they had to repeat the experiment. The same can be observed also for Dashboards B and D. Results also indicate that familiarity impacted adoption of visuals, as visuals with a low degree of familiarity tended to be less frequently adopted. As suggested by Ariely (2008), participants already developed a certain preference for what is familiar, even in a strikingly short period of time. The impact of familiarity is not surprising, because familiar visuals are not only easier to use, but they are also quick to use. Therefore, one should not underestimate the learning curve in the adoption of new visuals.

Thus, if familiar visuals (e.g., showing a hospital management report in a format that resembles a patient chart or using Sankey diagrams with engineering management) are purposeful and otherwise well designed, there is a strong argument to use them, because they are likely to be embraced by the decision makers (Figures 4.2, 4.13, and 4.18 exemplify such a combination of purposefulness and familiarity). New visuals should be introduced with care, since—as with any change—resistance is to be expected.

6. Although familiarity is critical, it should not hold back change. The effect of familiarity appears to be moderated by the degree to which visuals adhere to the design principles, as participants using Dashboard C were more prepared to abdicate familiarity and try new solutions. Thus, if the current visuals used in an organization are not well designed, one would expect a lower resistance to change. Moreover, the impact of familiarity in visual choices can be ameliorated if change is incremental (as discussed in point 3 above).

7. Some of the preferences for different visuals revealed enhanced visual literacy. A few participants understood the importance of different perspectives, took the time to understand them (effectively), and engaged with them in a phased approach (see summary in Section 6.8). Such skills are critical to improve the use of visuals, and hence to better utilize their potential.

8. User preference played an important role. Adoption was partly idiosyncratic. This reflects the diverse population of the experiment, with different interests, styles, and ways of thinking, and also their preferences for different visuals. Participants even had strong emotional reactions to visuals. Thus, regardless of literacy in the design and use of visuals, there will be always some disagreement, whether a visual is "good" or "bad," "liked" or "disliked," or found "useful" or "useless."

CHAPTER 7

Summary, Conclusions, and Recommendations

As stated in Chapter 1, the objective of this book was to increase awareness of the importance of visuals and to provide practical recommendations on how visuals can be used and designed in a mindful manner. Specifically, our empirical analysis explored the role of visuals to enhance cognition of data in decisions and proposed forms of visualization that encourage more informed decisions.

In order to capture the entirety of the visualization challenge in our research context, we explored four foundational areas: 1) project portfolio management (PPM) and more specifically decision making in the portfolio management context; 2) behavioral strategy; 3) organizational theory, especially the visual dimension of organizations; and 4) data visualization (i.e., the underlying disciplines of neuroscience and visual design).

PPM was deliberately chosen as the specific research context. It is complex and characterized by a dynamic, political decision process that typically involves one or multiple groups of decision makers, who periodically review, select, balance, and terminate projects. We define three types of complexity that impact PPM: 1) structural complexity, resulting from the large number of possible combinations of projects, interdependencies among projects, and different project types; 2) emergent complexity, due to the lack of information, the stochastic nature of future outcomes, changing goals and constraints, materialization of risks and opportunities, and unexpected events; and 3) sociopolitical complexity, due to multiple stakeholders, group dynamics, and multiple decision makers with different and changing objectives, as well as the complexity attributed to bounded rationality and irrationality.

If properly designed or selected, visuals can help address the complexity involved in portfolio decisions, in particular, its cognitive and communication challenges.

Visuals can be powerful cognition aids, as they impact the way we make sense of situations.[65] Visuals support sensemaking and hence decisions by offering and encouraging engagement with different perspectives on the multifaceted portfolio problem (e.g., portfolio balance, strategic alignment, maximization of financial value, identification of projects that do not meet threshold, etc.). They enable decision makers to more effectively process large amounts of data and solve problems quicker and more accurately. Visuals can improve clarity and are superior to textual information, because complex relationships can be understood more easily and quickly. For example, territories can be understood faster and with less error through the use of maps. The same applies for interdependencies, when network diagrams are used, as well as portfolio trade-offs, when displaying projects in bubble charts or scatterplots. Well-designed visuals can leverage our natural ability to rapidly recognize visual patterns.[66] Visuals can also extend the short-term memory, which is otherwise very limited. Therefore, visuals help cope with structural complexity and uncertainty, as well as lessen cognitive biases and hence address sociopolitical complexity.

Visuals also aid sensemaking because they facilitate communication. Visuals mediate negotiations, as they allow constructing and sharing interpretations and viewpoints. For example, a Gantt chart allows a portfolio board to easily navigate, evaluate, and negotiate timelines for various portfolio scenarios for interdependent projects. It is important to recognize that the visual used influences the negotiation process. For example, if, instead of a Gantt chart a stakeholder map is used, the focus of the conversation and negotiations could change considerably. Visuals also act as epistemic objects, that is, as a vehicle to store and share knowledge and as a form of organizational memory. A recent development in this area is the use of condensed visual stories, for instance, through highly condensed project status report dashboards, or other infographics. Visuals can create a space to invite alternative opinions, inspire thinking, challenge stakeholders, or convey passion to engage with or change the group dynamic. Lastly, as demonstrated by marketing and public relations, visuals also influence the image of organizations, individuals, or conditions and can be used to portray projects and investment opportunities in a certain light. This can increase or decrease their legitimacy. Hence, visuals address socio-political complexity and act as boundary objects that connect diverse interests and viewpoints.

However, visuals can be the source of accidental or deliberate deceit. Deceit can result from poorly constructed visuals (e.g., scale inconsistency, ambiguity,

---

[65] Sensemaking is an active, two-way, and iterative process through which people find or construct a story to account for the data in their own frame of reference, based on the information available to them, their goals, experience, convictions, commitment, emotions, and so on. Continuous try-out of new frames and reframing takes place, especially in a group setting: Negotiating and group sensemaking set in.

[66] See Section 4.6.3, and in particular Table 4.3 for more information about our natural visual skills.

and other design flaws) but also from more subtle mechanisms to stress certain
aspects of the situation over others.

Many types of visuals are currently used in PPM, for example, bubble charts, treemaps, heatmaps, Gantt charts and calendar charts, portfolio funnels, portfolio tables, roadmaps, network diagrams, efficient frontier graphs, decision trees, and others. Although certain types of visuals are reoccurring in the literature and in practice, there is little awareness of the importance of designing or selecting the best possible visual for the task at hand. Hence, learning more about how visuals impact our thinking, communication, and action is critical to project and portfolio management.

Enhancing visual literacy involves the development of three competencies: 1) the ability to *design* visuals (i.e., to consciously produce, compose, and create visual messages); 2) the ability to *use* them effectively; and 3) the awareness of the importance of *user and designer* idiosyncrasies, such as experience, familiarity, and emotional reactions to visuals.

This research provides guidance to improve visual literacy. It focuses on how visuals impact the cognition of data in portfolio decisions and how to use and design visuals to support cognition in this context. Answering this question is critical for exploiting the potential that visuals have in the PPM context, and for improving consciousness in their use and design.

The question was addressed through a literature review and our empirical research experiment. The literature review revealed how visuals impact cognition (see Chapter 3, and the above summary) and defined the guiding principles, which suggests approaches for the use and design of visuals (see Section 4.6 and Table 7.1).

The conclusions from our literature review and experiences were translated into research propositions that were tested through a human subject experiment with 204 UCL students. The participants of the experiment were asked to select a project portfolio for a company with 16 projects available for consideration, a strategy statement from the CEO, a set of defined goals (e.g., short- and long-term ROI, confidence of success, degree of innovation), and constraints (e.g., funds and personnel resources). Participants made the decision based on different dashboards constructed with varying degrees of adherence to our design principles. Table 7.2 summarizes the empirical results.

7.1 Implications for Practitioners

This book highlights the importance of visuals in the context of sensemaking and decisions and illustrates it within the portfolio management context. We believe that the notions conveyed apply to project management generally, and that the proposed principles hold true beyond the specific PPM context.

For practitioners, it is critical to develop an awareness of what makes visuals effective as a cognition and communication aid. In order to do so, there is a need to develop the ability to use, select, or design effective visuals. This will help practitioners to convincingly present proposed projects, effectively convey risks, and outline dependencies in their full detail.

Table 7.1—Overview of design principles.

Principle	Definition	Rational and Theoretical Underpinning	Relevance to Practice
Interactive	A visual is interactive if it allows users to change and organize data and parameters within an established structure.	The principle is based on a paradigm shift in data visualization, moving the focus from producing and disseminating to using and interacting with information.	Interactive visuals enable the user to think and probe ideas through the visuals (i.e., to organize, reorganize, and look at data from different perspectives, and thereby enhance understanding of the problem).
Purposeful	A visual is purposeful if it addresses at least one relevant perspective of a portfolio problem.	1) Cognition fit theory: different cognitive tasks are more effectively displayed by different visuals. 2) Project portfolios are a multifaceted problem. They demand different perspectives and cognitive tasks. Hence, there is a need for combination of purposeful visuals.	Purposeful visuals enable the analysis of different perspectives of portfolio problems, such as trade-offs, interdependencies, strategic alignment, stakeholder support, and so forth. Use of a combination of purposeful visuals can therefore help reduce mistakes and ensure analysis of most relevant perspectives.
Truthful	A visual is truthful if it displays relevant data accurately.	Visual design is based on the translation from a referent (data, concepts, ideas, etc.) to a physical representation (the visual). This is the key source of deceit and persuasion mechanisms.	Whether consciously or not, visuals can deceive. This can result from poorly constructed visuals (e.g., scale inconsistency) and also from more subtle mechanisms, such as filtering data, creating different emphasis, and evoking an image that does not represent the "reality" (e.g., more precise, more mature, etc.). Understanding these mechanisms is key to recognize, avoid, and consciously (and we hope also ethically) use them.
Efficient	Efficient visuals take advantage of our natural ability to interpret visuals. They mindfully display the maximum amount of information in the smallest space possible, so the visual can be processed rapidly and accurately.	Our cognition is limited, but our visual system is a very powerful cognition aid, particularly if visuals consider humans' natural pattern recognition skills (Gestalt law and pre-attentive processes of visual cognition), use space mindfully, combine different purposes, and use redundancy mindfully.	Efficient visuals tap into the potential of our visual system to enhance our ability to think quicker and sharper.
Aesthetic	A visual is aesthetic if it is perceived as harmonious, professional, and beautiful.	Research on working spaces and service quality draws attention to well-being and images of legitimacy and professionalism in the workplace. Aesthetics of visuals can also influence portfolio contexts for the same reasons.	Aesthetic visuals can be considered more trustworthy, improve usability and adoption, and recognize a rather emotional connection with workplace and business tools (among them, visuals).

Portfolios and large projects can exhibit a degree of complexity that easily exceeds the human ability to grasp the complete context and environment and consider all its relevant aspects. Effective visuals can "lower the bar," reduce complexity, and enable improved cognition. This book provides numerous examples and illustrations on how to do so.

A set of practical recommendations for designing and using visuals generally and specifically for PPM has been established, namely the following:

- Design visuals carefully
  - Purposeful and interactive visuals enhance cognition of data and decision quality and lead to more consistent results across audiences, especially if the team is rather heterogeneous. Efficiency and truthfulness are also useful to improve cognition and decision quality.
  - Not following the stated design principles at all can have a negative impact on the cognition of data and ultimately the decision, and can also lead to lower levels of adoption.
  - Better designs will not necessarily make people more confident in their decisions. Aligning adherence to principles and familiarity with

Table 7.2—Summary of findings. **115**

How can the use and design of visuals support cognition of data in project portfolio decisions?			
	Proposition and questions	**Variables and methods**	**Findings**
Design	**Proposition 1a:** Cognition of data is positively influenced by adherence to design principles (interactive, purposeful, and supporting).	Cognition: decision quality (number of mistakes and strategic fit score)	Partly supported. Dashboard A (interactive) and B (purposeful) led to the highest reduction in number of mistakes, followed by Dashboard D (supporting). Dashboard C (not following principles) led to significantly inferior decisions. Yet no significant impact on confidence was observed. The same was observed after an improvement on visual design. This suggests that adhering to design principles contributed to an improvement in decision quality, in particular interactive and purposeful principles, while not inducing overconfidence.
	Proposition 1b: Confidence is positively influenced by adherence to design principles (interactive, purposeful, and supporting).	Confidence: confidence in decision controlled by overall confidence	
	Proposition 1c: Despite negative implications of change (e.g., adoption problems, learning curve), improvement on visual design positively impacts cognition of data.	Visual design: four dashboards with different degrees of adherence to design principles (interactive, purposeful, and supporting)	
Use	**Proposition 2a:** There is a nonlinear relationship between the number of visuals used and cognition of data.	Use: number and choice of visuals used	Partly supported. Indicative support for the impact of choice of visuals in decision quality (in particular, reduction of mistakes). Number of visuals used significantly impacts confidence but not decision quality (i.e., they can lead to higher degree of confidence, regardless of whether the decision quality has improved).
	Proposition 2b: The use of more visuals contributes to an increase in confidence and can lead to overconfidence.		
User	**Proposition 3a:** Cognition is positively influenced by familiarity with the visuals used.	Visual experience: familiarity	Partly supported. Familiarity significantly impacts confidence but not decision quality. Familiarity also played an important role in adoption and preferences of dashboards.
	Proposition 3b: Confidence is positively influenced by familiarity with the visuals used.		
Relationship	**Proposition 4:** There is a correlation between design, use, and user.	Same as above	Not supported. Participants did not engage with several visuals, not even when the visuals adhered to design principles and were purposeful. There is some indication that low familiarity could explain this result.
Questions	**Question 1:** How do people use visuals skills?	Open questions in the post-experimental survey and interview	Understand what visuals to use, why, how, and when, both for familiar and unfamiliar visuals.
	Question 2: How do people react to different visuals (visual preferences and adoption)?	Same as above	Dashboard A (interactive) and B (purposeful) were preferred, followed by D (supporting), confirming the importance of visual design principles. Few visuals were used. Adoption increased when: • visuals adhere to design principles; • visuals are perceived as easy, comprehensive, relevant, precise, interactive, and quick to interpret; • visuals are required, not only helpful; • visuals are familiar, yet this is moderated by the degree to which visuals adhere to the design principles (the worse the current visual, the higher the adoption of improved visuals), and when less familiar and less used visuals are added to familiar visuals; • participants had choices of visuals, and perceived a visual as a "free option;" • participants were visually literate; and • participants "liked" it (individual preference matters).

visuals can help increase confidence and decision quality, and should be preferred, when possible.

- Even if visuals are well designed, there is a need to introduce new visuals carefully, and to mind the potential learning curve necessary for the visuals to be used effectively.

- Adoption of new visuals can be increased if the visuals: adhere to design principles; are perceived as easy to use, comprehensive, relevant, and precise; are interactive and quick to interpret; are required and not only helpful; and are familiar (but also purposeful).
- Use visuals consciously
  - Ensure that visuals address the critical perspectives of the problem.
  - However, be selective: A lack of visuals will limit understanding; too many visuals can overwhelm and lead to overconfidence.
  - Use purposeful visuals, and—when possible—use visuals that combine different perspectives.
  - Consider which visuals to use, how, why, and when, and do not hesitate to use unfamiliar visuals if they are purposeful. This practice will enhance visual literacy with time.
  - Visuals are persuasion mechanisms. Engage with them critically. Consider, for example: What data have been filtered out? Which perspectives does the visual show and not show? What interests does the visual represent?
- Mind the user
  - Use familiar visuals for difficult topics where you would like to enhance people's confidence in the decision, improving adoption.
  - People prefer familiar over well-designed visuals; hence, well-designed visuals are not necessarily an "easy sell."
  - Provide different visuals showing different perspectives of the problem, yet don't expect everyone to understand and engage with every visual, and bear in mind that too many options can distract rather than help.
  - Allow time and explain unusual visuals.
  - Listen to users and adapt visuals accordingly—some people have valuable intuitive visual skills.
- Manage change of visuals carefully
  - Changing to better-designed visuals is worthwhile—it improves decision quality.
  - Yet, there is not necessarily an impact on confidence levels.
- Confidence and decision quality are not strongly related. Be careful. Your confidence in a decision is not an indicator of good quality; overconfidence is common, particularly when using a larger number of familiar visuals.

Therefore, it is of key importance to educate decision makers, project management, and project team members on how to use visuals in a mindful manner. As common sense suggests, a map in the hands of two different people navigating unknown territory may lead to different outcomes. The same applies to project and portfolio charts. An educated decision maker who understands both the capabilities and potential limitations (e.g., distortions or deceit) of a particular visual can think more sharply and quickly.

7.2   Implications for Teaching and Learning

As the project management profession pays more and more attention to skills beyond the tools of the trade (i.e., the Knowledge Areas of the *PMBOK® Guide*), those skills that improve cognition and communication become increasingly important. This applies even more as project managers are exposed to larger and more complex stakeholder groups; hence, presenting information with impact becomes increasingly important.

As this and other research efforts have demonstrated, visuals matter and aid cognition and communication. Therefore, they should be addressed mindfully in project and portfolio teaching and learning. This research provides a comprehensive overview of the impact of visuals in the way we think, communicate, and act. In this respect, integration of knowledge has been one of our key efforts (Boyer, 1994). Therefore, the book also serves as a starting point for those new to this the topic and to the design of teaching and learning material that enhances visual literacy in project and portfolio management.

7.3   Implications for Research

7.3.1 Contributions

The most relevant contribution of this research is that it markedly advances our knowledge of visuals and visual literacy in the project and portfolio context and literature.

There has been some research in project management and PPM literature (Killen, 2013; Taxén & Lilliesköld, 2008), yet previous studies focused on visualizing interdependencies. This is critical, but represents only one of the many potential contributions of visuals to improving cognition and decision making in project and portfolio management. Moreover, previous research fell short in addressing the broader literature in data visualization and in organizational theory. A strong link with theory and theorizing had yet to be established. We have both provided a more holistic account of the impact of visuals in how we act, think, and communicate, and have done so using a theoretical lens, namely sensemaking. We have also made some progress in theorizing about the role of visuals in our context, through our propositions and their empirical validation.

There is also insightful research exploring the role of visuals in project contexts, particularly in construction projects. We would like to draw readers' attention to the work of Yakura (2002, 2013), Justesen and Mouritsen (2009), and Whyte and colleagues (e.g., Ewenstein & Whyte, 2009; Whyte et al., 2008). Yet most of the publications are outside of classic project management journals. We explicitly bring these publications to the project management literature and their insights to recommendations for project and portfolio management practice.

In particular, we have advanced knowledge by proposing and validating design principles, which draw on both organizational theory and data visualization. Our empirical research also indicates that visuals have different impacts on decision quality and confidence. Although our research concluded that visual design impacts decision quality, and has no significant impact on confidence, the number of visuals used and their familiarity increases confidence, but has no significant impact on decision quality.

A further contribution of this research bridges two research fields that were until now mostly disconnected: data visualization and organization theory (the visual dimension, in particular), and, specifically, bringing data visualization concepts to organization theory and project management.[67] This connection is pertinent because organizational theory mainly focuses on the impact of visuals as communication aids, while data visualization draws particular attention to visuals as cognition aids. Although the focus of our empirical research has been on cognition, we connected these two facets in our literature review and discussed their relationships. We also contextualized them by drawing implications to address the complexities of project portfolio decisions. We therefore added a focus on individual cognition to organizational theory. This is relevant to the development of managers' visual literacy, and leads to a wider understanding of the role of visuals in our thinking.

Bridging these two fields was also insightful because concepts from data visualization, and from the semiology of graphics, have helped us articulate how visuals function and why they act differently from verbal communication. This has served as the foundation to our discussions of visuals as communication and cognition aids. To our knowledge, this link has not been made as explicitly and holistically in previous research.

The research also contributes to data visualization literature, which focuses on simple experiments and mainly on how people engage with visuals. In our experiment, we simulated a complex context, which allowed us to explore more complex individual behaviors over a longer period of time,[68] such as the role of familiarity developed in the course of the experiment. It also helped us validate the impact of visuals in the cognition of more complex problems.

Furthermore, decisions in the project portfolio context have been given little attention in research. Our effort has contributed to the academic conversation: 1) by providing a holistic understanding of portfolio decisions in the context of the sensemaking process, and 2) by discussing and empirically validating how visuals can influence this process.

Finally, we aspired to make a contribution to bridge theory and practice in this particular area, and to reconcile academic rigor and practical relevance. This has been at the heart of the research, from the composition of the research team, which included both academic and practitioners' perspectives. Reconciling research and practice is extremely arduous. Although we recognize that this book is more academic in nature, the research in itself has a strong practical focus, namely as a validation of design principles and our aim to raise awareness and knowledge among project and portfolio managers about visuals.

---

[67] A full account of how we built this bridge is published elsewhere (Geraldi & Arlt, 2013).

[68] For experimental setup, 45 minutes to an hour working on a single task is long.

7.3.2 Limitations

Limitations of the research were discussed in Section 5.7. The key limitation of the research design was the unexpected heterogeneity of the participant population in regard to their problem-solving ability, which is partly useful, as it represents heterogeneity in practice, yet led to methodological difficulties and sample size problems for some analysis. In addition, design judgments are subjective and introduce potential distortions, as for example, a visual may be more or less purposeful than intended, even if design criteria were adhered to. Moreover, because participants also engaged with a limited number of visuals, the nonlinear relationship between number of visuals used and cognition of data, Proposition 2a, could not be empirically validated. Lastly, generalizing the findings of the experiment for decisions beyond the PPM context is problematic, given the specific scope of the experiment. These limitations are one aspect that leads to the need for further research, which will be discussed in the next section.

7.3.3 Future Research

Research in project and portfolio contexts mainly studies and draws on verbal language data. There is a growing body of literature—including this research—that demonstrates the relevance of visuals to management practices in general and to the project and portfolio management contexts in particular. Therefore, there is a need to include visuals both as a relevant research topic and as a source of empirical data in project management research.

This call has been already acknowledged in general management, and one can observe emerging conversations in the area, including the visual dimension, but also objects and space, as visuals can be seen as a working space. Just as an illustration, the 2014 Academy of Management Conference called for contributions on the role of language in management, and explicitly mentioned visual language. The role of visuals as a valid and important source of data in research has also been acknowledged in management research methods, most notably by inVisio, an ESRC-funded research,[69] which has developed into an international network for visual studies in organizations. Yet, research efforts in project and portfolio contexts have been scant.

Based on the results and limitations of this research, we suggest further exploring and developing the following:

- Similar questions and propositions of our research effort, but in different experimental setups, for example:
  - The decision task used in the experiment involves a portfolio of 16 projects. What would have happened if we had a more complex decision task, with a hundred or more projects, where lists are ineffective and other visuals become critical?

---

[69] Economic & Social Research Council, the largest social science funding body in the United Kingdom.

- Dashboards were not consciously deceptive. It would be interesting to explore the impact of visuals that attempted to lead participants to certain decisions. Would that impact the decisions? Would it impact confidence? Would the participants notice it? If so, which implications would it have in the way they engaged with the visuals, in their perceptions about the experiment, and so forth?
  - The experiment focused on individual decisions; future research can explore the role of visuals in group decisions.
- A contingent understanding of the impact of visuals across different types of projects and portfolios:
  - Though generic guiding principles were proposed, we do not suggest that the visuals designed for one context would be applicable to others. To the contrary, the purposeful principle states that visuals need to display the different and relevant perspectives of the problem at hand. As the problem changes, so do the perspectives and hence the visuals to be used. Therefore, in order to use visuals mindfully and follow the principles suggested in this research, there is a need to improve our understanding of the relevant perspectives across different contexts, and how they can be best visualized. Future research could explore the difference in the use and design of visuals for project portfolios with higher structural complexity versus those inherently uncertain and dynamic, versus those that are particularly political.
  - In this line, our research has focused on the role of visuals in project portfolio decisions. Further studies could explore the role of visuals in project and program contexts.
- The relationship between number of visuals, confidence, and cognition could be explored sin more depth (e.g., would it be moderated by good visual design?). In other words, when visuals are not purposeful, they provide the *impression* of engaging with a larger amount of information without providing additional perspectives on the problem. Would people be less likely to become overconfident if they used a large number of purposeful visuals instead of visuals that are not purposeful?
- Further study of the relationship between familiarity, confidence, and cognition, particularly over longer periods of time (e.g., does knowing a visual contribute to overconfidence in the long term?), could be useful. Maybe the increasing use and familiarity with a visual will also lead to a better understanding of its limitations (learning effects will occur) and confidence in the interpretation of a visual may go down again to realistic levels, and hence overconfidence will be avoided. On the other hand, would the existence of familiar visuals encourage decision makers to gravitate toward familiar visuals, and with that, also familiar perspectives of the problem? If this is correct, than the familiar visuals would bias the decision, and develop a less accurate understanding of the problem. This could contribute to overconfidence, as decision makers have the *impression* that the situation is familiar (same visuals, same perspectives, similar interpretations), yet in reality new perspectives would have been advantageous.

- Focus on the actual design and use of visuals in portfolio decisions both in individual and groups in organizations could include:
  - The role of visuals in cognition and in particular as frames in the sensemaking process, for example:
    - ○ Which perspectives are most visible in projects, and which ones are particularly hidden or "invisible"? Why? Is it a conscious choice?
    - ○ How many visuals are used in a portfolio decision? Project report? Meetings? Are they really adding to cognition and communication of information or are they rather overwhelming and potentially leading to overconfidence?
  - The role of visuals as communication aids, for example:
    - ○ When do project managers use visuals? To what extent do they do it consciously?
    - ○ How can visuals be used to shape sensemaking processes? Which visuals are typically used? What are the specific impacts of different visuals in this process? Do project and portfolio managers use them consciously? What happens if one deliberately changes it to a different perspective?
    - ○ How can visuals act as boundary objects connecting different perspectives if different stakeholder groups are likely to be familiar with different visuals, and familiarity plays an important role in the adoption and confident use of visuals?
    - ○ How is filtering of data and information used for persuasion, and also as a mechanism to communicate with different audiences, and what are its implications on ethics?
    - ○ How are visuals used as epistemic objects in projects and with what effects on organizational learning, memory, and knowledge management? Could it reduce the "cost of knowledge" with quicker assimilation of knowledge through, for instance, condensed visual formats such as infographics?
    - ○ How do project actors use visuals to tell stories and convey metaphors? Do they? Why? With what effects?
  - The role of visuals in the interface between temporary and standing organizations:
    - ○ Temporary and standing organizations have different perspectives on projects and their role. Can visuals act as boundary objects connecting this link?

Regarding the PPM area, we contend that current research in portfolio management is still dominated by normative guidance from the 1990s. We therefore join Martinsuo (2013) and Petit and Hobbs (2010) in a call to broaden our understanding of project portfolios and reconnect research with the actual portfolio practices. In particular, we suggest further research that explores decisions in projects and portfolio contexts. Specifically, there is a need to expand work in the area and improve and strengthen its connection with decision theory, and the emerging area of behavior strategy. Given the context of projects as temporary organizations and portfolios as a bridge between temporary and permanent organizations, the behaviors and dynamics of decision making and sensemaking are likely to be different, and hence, there is a potential to contribute not only to project management literature but also to general management and decision theory.

Finally, the research has been innovative in terms of its methodology. Experimental research is still underexplored in project management research (with notable exceptions, e.g., Arlt, 2010; Gersick, 1988; Harrison & Harrell, 1993; Killen, 2013). Yet it is a powerful methodology to address certain types of research questions, such as individual and group behaviors in temporary organizations, which can be simulated in experimental settings well. Therefore, we endorse such a methodology for such research in the future.

7.4   Toward a Mindful Use of Visuals

Visuals have become an integral part of how we manage projects and portfolios. They impact our thinking, communication, and actions. In short, visuals matter! To tap into their potential, mindful use and design of visuals is required. Throughout this book, we have discussed and studied how visuals function and how we function with visuals. This work resulted in advancement of knowledge and practical guidance to enhance our understanding of visuals in project and portfolio decisions.

Above all, visuals are about people, as they are made by people and for people. We hope our efforts will increase the awareness of the importance of visuals and encourage their mindful design and use in practice and in research.

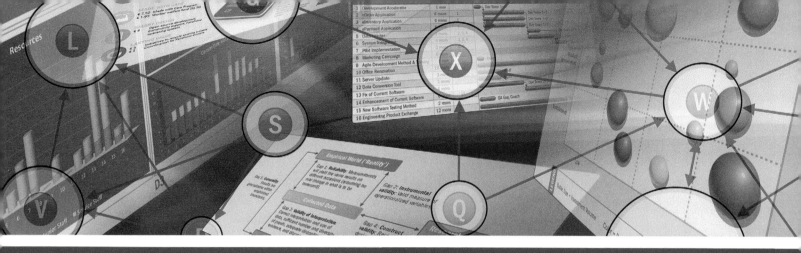

CHAPTER 8

Appendices

Appendix A: Historical Overview and Current Trends in the Literature

Visuals are created for a multitude of purposes in many disciplines. Their development is intertwined with the different problems they attempt to address (Beniger & Robyn, 1978; Friendly & Denis, 2001), and their effects in society (Mitchell, 1994) and in organizations (Meyer et al., 2013). Consequently, literature about visuals has been mostly contextual and fragmented across scientific disciplines (e.g., medicine, astronomy, cartography, etc.).

However, in the last years, data visualization has established itself as a research field of its own. Since then, increasingly comprehensive historical accounts and an integrative and cross-disciplinary body of knowledge have been developed.[70] Such work helped in the creation of a common language and memory of the emerging discipline. It also contributed to the cross-fertilization of ideas among disciplines and the development of generic principles of data visualization.

A parallel development has been the growing body of work on the implications of visuals and a visual rhetoric. This work emerged in the social sciences and humanities, in areas such as art history, film and media studies, sociology, and organization theory. This new and emerging knowledge area still lacks a definitive label. Here it is called visual dimension, in line with organization theory terminology.

---

[70] Friendly and Denis's (2001) milestone project is notable here. The work summarizes key developments on data visualization and is publicly available at www.datavis.ca/milestones/

Although visuals can be inspired and informed by general principles and concepts, visual solutions remain contextual. In this respect, visuals emerge in the intersection between generic developments in data visualization/visual dimension, and custom-developed solutions that are based on an in-depth understanding of specific problems and the potential role of visuals in addressing them.

Throughout this book, we have focused on the application of generic ideas of data visualization to the portfolio context. This section will address the generic part of the discipline. It presents a brief account of the history of visuals, its key milestones, and current streams of thinking. The first section focuses on the data visualization literature and the second on the visual dimension.

A.1. Visual-Driven Perspective

The history of visuals goes back quite a long time. As of today, the first known map dates as far back as 16,500 BC and consists of a map of parts of the sky (Whitehouse, 2000). The point here is not to establish a clear origin of the use and creation of visuals in human history. However, to realize that visuals predate virtually all other forms of written communication and have been used for cognition and communication in humanity's earliest records is noteworthy.

With time, the use of visuals became increasingly elaborate, such as the Egyptian surveyors' use of the coordinate system in 1,500 BC, the medieval astronomers' representations of the sky in the 10th century[71], musical notes that have been represented as time series since around the 13th century, or Leonardo da Vinci's images of the motion of the human arm in the 14th century.

However, it was not until the end of the 18th century that the potential of graphics became significantly prevalent and visual representations became commonplace in the Western world. The 19th century can be considered visualization's "Age of Enthusiasm" (Palsky, 1996, in Friendly & Denis, 2001), due to an explosive growth in statistical graphics and thematic mappings, and a wealth of innovations in the design of visuals, including histograms, time-series plots, contour plots, thematic cartography (Friendly & Denis, 2001), and the recognition of visual representations as a cognition aid across scientific publications (Beniger & Robyn, 1978).

An exemplary visual of this period is Figure A.1[72]:

Popularized by Tufte (2001), Minard's map (Figure A.2) admirably tells the tragic story of Napoleon's march to Moscow in 1812 through a purposeful and rich visual representation. The visual uses a large number of variables neatly organized in a plot, namely temperature, time, size of the army, exact army

---

[71] Such representations are very much similar to those used today!

[72] See Friendly and Denis (2001) for a comprehensive list.

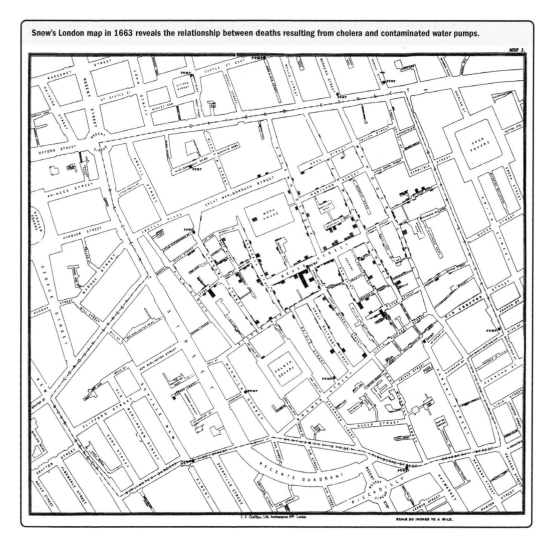

Snow's London map in 1663 reveals the relationship between deaths resulting from cholera and contaminated water pumps.

Figure A.1—Snow (1854): Cholera cases are highlighted in black (Snow's London map in 1663 reveals the relationship between deaths resulting from cholera and contaminated water pumps). Retrieved from http://matrix.msu.edu/~johnsnow/images/online_companion/chapter_images/fig12-5.jpg

location coordinates in different periods (latitude and longitude), and direction in which the army was traveling (see Figure 3.3).[73]

In the early 20th century, the use of visual representations continued to develop, yet at a slower pace. Scientific research focused on exact numbers and formal models that were not visible with graphics, and so the enthusiasm around visuals reduced dramatically. Yet, at that time, visuals were popularized in textbooks and became mainstream (Friendly & Denis, 2001).

---

[73] However, as discussed extensively in Section 4.6, Minard's visual was also criticized for being too complex, and so its message does not spring into mind as one gazes at it (Few, 2006). We contend that not all visuals need to be understood in the blink of eye. In this case, the visual is telling a story, not advising of an imminent dangerous situation. It is part of visual literacy to be able to engage and understand more complex visuals, as well as to produce them purposefully (i.e., recognizing different needs in the speed of pattern recognition, for instance).

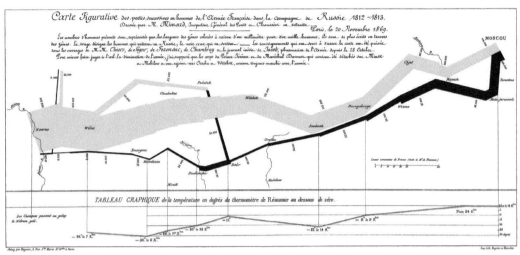

Charles Minard's 1869 chart showing the number of men in Napoleon's 1812 Russian campaign army, their movements, as well as the temperature they encountered on the return path. Lithograph, 62 x 30 cm, retrieved from http://en.wikipedia.org/wiki/File:Minard.png#metadata

Figure A.2—Example of visual display of complex information.

The development gathered pace from the mid-20th century, and was particularly aided by the rise of personal computing. Noteworthy contributions include the following:

- Huff's seminal book *How to Lie with Statistics*, published in 1954, demonstrated the deceiving nature of visual representations (Steele, 2005).
- Bertin's *Semiology of Graphics*, first published in 1967, called attention to the rules of visual perception that can be applied to graphics so they are intuitive, clear, accurate, and efficient (Few, 2010).
- Tukey developed the exploratory data analysis method (EDA) based on simple but effective graphics to improve understanding of statistical data in the 1960s (Friendly & Denis, 2001).[74]
- Tufte's *Visual Display of Quantitative Information*, published in 1983, is a landmark in the development of visual representations. His subsequent publications, such as *Envisioning Information* and *Beautiful Evidence*, are also recognized as classics in the field. The author proposes principles for insightful graphics, emphasizing the accuracy of visual representation (exact display of the data) and efficiency (minimalist display of data, increasing the data-ink ratio).

From the 1980s and onward, the field bloomed. In the 1990s, data visualization became a research field of its own[75] and since 2000 the field has experienced a breakthrough. Owing to the increasing complexity and volume of data

---

[74] Tukey proposed the method in a seminal article called "The Future of Statistics" published in 1962. The ideas gained recognition in the 1970s, and were summarized in his book published in 1977 (Friendly & Denis, 2001).

[75] See a collection of the best articles at the time in Card, Mackinlay, and Shneiderman (1999).

available,[76] and to massive developments in processing power and computer graphics,[77] visuals have gained more attention and become even more critical and helpful.

Top management has given increased attention to data (and visuals) as they realize the potential of business analytics (Davenport, 2006) and big data (e.g., LaValle, Lesser, Shockley, Hopkins, & Kruschwitz, 2011; McAfee, Brynjolfsson, Davenport, Patil, & Barton, 2012) as sources of meaningful information to guide decisions and action in organizations.

This boost of interest has led to creative new arrangements of data.[78] McCandless (2009) presents excellent examples of this development in the myriad of visual representations. Yet, new visuals are not only present in specialized publications, but become more and more available in everyday life, be it infographics such as Toyota's A3 report, which provides an overview of the project plan and progress in one page, or the overview of contacts on LinkedIn (the professional social network), or in presentations from TED (Technology, Entertainment, Design is a nonprofit organization devoted to "ideas worth spreading"; see http://www.ted.com/).

Improved algorithms and enhanced computational and computer graphics performance enabled sophisticated technologies like AlloSphere,[79] a 3-D immersive theater in Santa Barbara, California, where scientists can interact with research data and, for example, "enter" a 3-D model of the brain. Technology (e.g., display technology and processing power) continues to improve rapidly. This allows for new visualization approaches, such as the overlaying of real-world environments with data representations, also known as augmented reality.

Furthermore, intuitive interfaces have made the design of visuals accessible to a wider range of people, and users are also becoming visual designers. Today anyone can explore large data sets and utilize a broad range of highly customized visual representations. There are also several tools to create visual representations available to the public, such as Google News Map, an application to visualize news using treemaps, and numerous sites such as Infogr.am, Tableau Public, VIDI, and others[80].

---

[76] Just as an illustration, Global IP traffic increased from 100 gigabytes (GB) per day in 1992 to 16,144 GB per second in 2014, and is estimated to surpass the zettabyte (1,000 exabytes) threshold by the end of 2016 (Cisco, 2015).

[77] Visualization was seen as a subfield of computer graphics, because computer graphics often render the engine to develop visualizations, and both share similar tools, concepts, and techniques. However, they have very different goals. Whereas visualization is aimed at sensemaking and communication of data, computer graphics are typically used to develop iterative synthetic images and animations, often three-dimensional (Ward et al., 2010).

[78] Many of these innovations were driven by the design and art community, and can be grouped into a new area of research that combines visualization techniques and principles of creative design—information aesthetics (Lau & Moere, 2007).

[79] See www.allosphere.ucsb.edu/

[80] There are plenty of tools available; see, e.g., Machlis's review in *Computerworld* (http://www.computerworld.com/article/2506820/business-intelligence/business-intelligence-chart-and-image-gallery-30-free-tools-for-data-visualization-and-analysis.html?nsdr=true). Yet, bear in mind that the field is dynamic; therefore, such reviews become rapidly dated. For example, IBM's ManyEyes initiative, an experimental online tool that allows many forms of visual exploration of data, closed in June 2015.

VISUALS MATTER!

Sociologists, art historians, and communication scientists provide a different approach to developing visuals than data visualization scholars do. While data visualization was mainly focused on how visuals can be used for cognition, sociologists' interests lie in the role of data visualization on society. Such a perspective is particularly relevant because it unravels the more critical, political, and behavioral aspects of visualization, all of which are pivotal to our engagement with visuals in project portfolio decisions and in organizations in general.

Jeremy Bentham's concept of the panopticon, Lacan's concept of the gaze, and Foucault's interpretation of surveillance as a source of power are all notable examples of some of the early work in the area of visual dimension. However, only in recent decades have visuals have become increasingly prevalent in our society, and reflection about visuals has become more common in the humanities and social sciences. Recently, new interdisciplinary fields of work around visuals have formed, such as visual culture and media studies. In the past few years, there has also been an emerging conversation among organization theorists (see review in Meyer et al., 2013).

Some research in the area is focused on the differences between visual and written text as different types of language, and hence, as a different rhetoric. An interesting study reveals a change in visual rhetoric in the past century. Visuals used to be dedicated to represent the past, as a way to maintain power relations and perpetuate images of powerful and rich citizens. From the early to the mid-20th century, visual influence changed, and became most prevalent in advertising. Unlike oil paintings, visuals used in advertising provide an image of the future, and an embedded promise of change. In other words, the image seduces potential consumers and sells an idea of what the future might look like if one were to buy X or Y (see Berger, 1972, and the respective documentary, *Ways of Seeing*).

Much research on visual rhetoric derives from studies of advertising. It shows how powerful visual rhetoric is, and also how inherently different it is from text (see, e.g., Foss, 2004; Phillips & McQuarrie, 2004).

These studies have been of critical importance for an enhanced understanding of visuals. In particular, the rhetoric of advertising has brought us a long way in understanding visuals as an object of persuasion. Because they act on the subconscious level and connect with our emotions, visuals are a source of power, which can be used as much to enlighten as to manipulate. A further area of sociological inquiry is how visuals can act as a cognition crutch. Complex knowledge and situations are transformed into easily digestible bits and simple visuals that can be understood without significant effort (infographics are a typical example). This encourages oversimplification and lack of reflection. Therefore, there is a pressing need for critical engagement with visuals.

This becomes even more important because visuals (and motion visuals) are not only in (explicit) advertisements; they are embedded in nearly all objects we encounter in our daily lives. Sociologists argue that the omnipresence of visuals both in our private and organizational lives marks a societal turn from text to pictures—what has been labeled the emergence of visual culture, or the pictorial turn (Mitchell, 1994).

In this respect, like any powerful artifact, visuals are about people using and designing them. As Umberto Eco (1979) urges:

> A democratic civilization will save itself only if it makes the language of the image into a stimulus for critical reflection—not an invitation for hypnosis. (p. 12)

Eco recognizes the need for visual literacy, and his words dovetail with the objective of this book, which is to help project practitioners critically and mindfully use and design visuals in their projects.

Appendix B: Validation of Relevant Perspectives for Portfolios

Table B.1 validates relevant perspectives for portfolio selection decisions, as it checks whether any other perspective becomes relevant as one examines the different tasks involved in the portfolio selection process.

Table B.1—Validation of perspectives in the portfolio selection process.

Portfolio Selection Phases	Activity	Perspective	Potential Visual
Prescreening	Eliminate projects that don't meet pre-defined portfolio criteria (thresholds)	Threshold-centric	Manually applied criteria, strategic focus, champion, feasibility study available
	Earmark mandatory projects	Across all perspectives	
Project Analysis	Understand business case for each project, that is: • expected benefits, • strategic contribution, and • required resources based on a set of common metrics (Archer & Ghasemzadeh, 2004)	Project-centric	Decision trees, uncertainty estimate, resource requirements estimate, and so on
	Review KPIs and other project specific metrics	Project-centric	
	Identify interdependencies with other projects	Interdependence-centric	
Portfolio Screening	Reject nonviable projects (e.g., excessive use of resources, insufficient benefits contribution, including interdependencies)	Threshold-centric Interdependence-centric (check impact on other projects)	Ad hoc techniques (e.g., profiles)
	Identify strategic options (e.g., either develop a new product line or change the current one) and their consequence on strategy and value creation	Interdependence-centric Strategic benefit-centric Alignment-centric	
Portfolio Selection (Alternative)	Balance of dimensions	Balance-centric	AHP (Analytic Hierarchy Process), constrained optimization, scoring models, constrained optimization
	Alignment with strategy	Alignment-centric	
	With as great a value as possible	Threshold/Parameter-centric	
	Within constraints	Threshold/Parameter-centric Timing-centric	
	Within interdependencies	Interdependence-centric	
Portfolio Adjustment	Tweak portfolio	All perspectives	Matrix displays, sensitivity analysis

Appendix C: Survey

Introduction

Appendix C summarizes the findings of a survey undertaken as part of this research effort. Specifically, the survey intended to develop a preliminary understanding of the topic, and in particular shed light on the following:

1) Understanding the actual use of visuals
   - What types of visuals are used
   - For what purpose
   - Do they meaningfully support decision making? If yes, how?
   - How consciously (or not) are visuals selected for a certain purpose?
2) Understanding the requirements for more meaningful and useful visualizations

The survey was advertised on the PMI website and the LinkedIn project and portfolio management groups. A total of 30 people completed the survey. Respondents came from different industries, and occupied a variety of project-related roles, including project and program managers, IT managers, and members of the PMO. Owing to the small sample size, the data were analyzed qualitatively.

Results

Phase in portfolio: Visuals were mostly used for the progress report.

Use of visuals: Traditional visuals were used the most, such as Gantt charts, bar charts, pie charts, and traffic lights. Very few used a *combination* of visuals!

Medium: Visuals were seen mostly on paper or PC (i.e., interactive or static). Not many used visuals on a flip chart or a wall—visual data analysis was therefore mostly an *individual act.*

Principles: All design principles proposed in this research were perceived as relevant; purposeful was the highest rated principle. There was a small difference between the expected and current quality of visuals measured by adherence to principles.

Objective: Participants used visuals mostly to search for patterns, establish relationships, and detect differences. Only about a third of participants used visuals for grouping and prioritizing. This is surprising because these tasks are relevant to reduce structural complexity, which usually characterizes project portfolios.

Adoption of new visuals: Visuals were adopted mostly when mandated, but also when offered, observed by others, or as a result of one's own choice.

Favorite visuals varied widely: The visual mentioned most frequently was the Gantt chart, which was used to control project portfolios (5 out of 30).

Improvement: Although there was a small gap between the expected and perceived quality score of visuals measured by adherence to principles, nearly all participants suggested improvements on the current visuals. Improvements were mainly related with the *organizational context* (including the availability of accurate, relevant, and timely data; use of standard visuals to improve comparisons; and a functional IT system that enables a more effective use and interaction of available data and eases the production of tailored and automatically generated and self-updating visuals).

Competencies: Some respondents demonstrated conscious use of visuals, aspiring for purposeful use both for individual analysis and communication with others and visual support to explore the detail and context of data.

Recommendations

The survey points to a potential *underutilization* of visuals in the management of project portfolios. In order to exploit the potential of visuals, organizations need to develop a context and competencies that foster mindful use and design of visuals. In terms of context, organizations need to invest in an enabling IT infrastructure and a culture that allows the sharing of accurate data. The aim here is to ensure effective collection and use of timely and reliable information through user-friendly, flexible, and interactive software. Attention should also be given to the development of standard visualizations that are simple and enable easy comparison and, with that, the use of stored data. Yet, this alone will not suffice. Managers need to become more aware of the potential of visuals. For example, the current focus appears to be on the individual analysis of data; there is an opportunity to intensify the use of visuals in communication. Moreover, visuals appear to be used for routine activities, mostly to control projects against the baseline. There is an opportunity to engage with visuals as a more sophisticated decision aid.

References

Amar, R., Eagan, J., & Stasko, J. (2005, October). *Low-level components of analytic activity in information visualization.* Paper presented at the INFOVIS 2005, IEEE Symposium on Information Visualization, Minneapolis, MN, USA.

Appelt, K. C., Milch, K. F., Handgraaf, M. J. J., & Weber, E. U. (2011). The decision making individual differences inventory and guidelines for the study of individual differences in judgment and decision-making research. *Judgment and Decision Making, 6*(3), 252–262.

Archer, N. P., & Ghasemzadeh, F. (1996). *Project portfolio selection techniques: A review and suggested integration approach.* Paper presented at the Innovation Research Working Group Working Paper No. 46, Hamilton, Ontario, Canada.

Archer, N. P., & Ghasemzadeh, F. (1999). An integrated framework for project portfolio selection. *International Journal of Project Management, 17*(4), 207–216.

Archer, N., & Ghasemzadeh, F. (2004). Project portfolio selection and management. In P. Morris & J. Pinto (Eds.), *The Wiley guide to managing projects* (pp. 237–255). Hoboken, NJ: John Wiley & Sons.

Ariely, D. (2008). *Predictably irrational.* New York, NY: HarperCollins Publishers.

Arlt, M. (2010). *Advancing the maturity of project portfolio management through methodology and metrics refinements.* (Doctoral dissertation). RMIT University, Melbourne, Australia.

Arlt, M. (2011). *Application of Experimental Research to Project Portfolio Management.* Proceedings of IRNOP 2012, Montreal, Canada.

Arnheim, R. (1954). *Art and visual perception: A psychology of the creative eye.* Oakland, CA: University of California Press.

Artto, K. A., & Dietrich, P. H. (2004). Strategic business management through multiple projects. In P. Morris & J. Pinto (Eds.), *The Wiley guide to managing projects* (pp. 144–176). Hoboken, NJ: John Wiley & Sons.

Artto, K. A., Martinsuo, M., & Aalto, T. (2001). *Project portfolio management: Strategic management through projects.* Helsinki, Finland: Project Management Association Finland.

Baker, F. W. (2012). Visual literacy. *Media literacy in the K–12 classroom* (pp. 41–71). ISTE (International Society for Technology in Education).

Ball, S. B., & Cech, P. A. (1996). Subject pool choice and treatment effects in economic laboratory research. *Research in Experimental Economics, 6*(3), 239–292.

Bazerman, M. H. (2009). *Judgment in managerial decision making* (7th ed.). Hoboken, NJ: John Wiley & Sons.

Beattie, V., & Jones, M. J. (1992). The use and abuse of graphs in annual reports: A theoretical framework and an empirical study. *Accounting and Business Research, 22*(88), 291–303.

Bell, E. (2012). Ways of seeing organisational death: A critical semiotic analysis of organisational memorialisation. *Visual Studies, 27*(1), 4–17.

134 Bell, E., Warren, S., & Schroeder, J. (2014). *The Routledge companion to visual organization*. New York, NY: Routledge.

Beniger, J. R., & Robyn, D. L. (1978). Quantitative graphics in statistics: A brief history. *The American Statistician, 32*(1), 1–11.

Berger, J. (1972). *Ways of seeing*. London, England: Penguin Books.

Bertin, J. (2010). *Semiology of graphics: Diagrams, networks, maps* (W. J. Berg, Trans.). Redlands, CA: ESRI Press. (Original work published in 1967)

Blichfeldt, B. S., & Eskerod, P. (2008). Project portfolio management, There's more to it than what management enacts. *International Journal of Project Management, 26*(4), 357–365.

Bourgeois III, L. J., & Eisenhardt, K. M. (1988). Strategic decision processes in high velocity environments: Four cases in the microcomputer industry. *Management Science, 34*(7), 816–835.

Boyer, E. (1994). Scholarship reconsidered: Priorities for a new century. In Rigby, G. (Ed.), *Universities in the twenty-first century: A lecture series*. London, England: National Commission on Education.

Brill, J. M., Kim, D., & Branch, R. M. (2000). *Visual literacy defined: The results of a Delphi study: Can IVLA (operationally) define visual literacy?* Paper presented at the International Visual Literacy Association, Ames, IA, USA.

Bristor, V. J., & Drake, S. V. (1994). Linking the language arts and content areas through visual technology. *T. H. E. Journal, 22*(2), 74–77.

Bruine de Bruin, W., Parker, A. M., & Fischhoff, B. (2007). Individual differences in adult decision-making competence. *Journal of Personality and Social Psychology, 92*, 938–956.

Burri, R. V. (2012). Visual rationalities: Towards a sociology of images. *Current Sociology, 60*(1), 45–60.

Cable, J. H., Ordonez, J. F., Chintalapani, G., & Plainsant, C. (2004). *Project portfolio earned value management using treemaps*. Paper presented at the PMI Research Conference, London, England.

Card, S. K., Mackinlay, J. D., & Shneiderman, B. (1999). *Readings in information visualization: Using vision to think*. San Diego, CA: Academic Press.

Caron, F., Fumagalli, M., & Rigamonti, A. (2007). Engineering and contracting projects: A value at risk based approach to portfolio balancing. *International Journal of Project Management, 25*(6), 569–578.

Carroll, R. T. (2014, September 12). *Confirmation bias*. Retrieved from http://skepdic.com/confirmbias.html

Cisco. (2015). *The zettabyte era: Trends and analysis*. Retrieved from http://www.cisco.com/c/en/us/solutions/collateral/service-provider/visual-networking-index-vni/VNI_Hyperconnectivity_WP.pdf

Cohen, M. D., March, J. G., & Olsen, J. P. (1972). A garbage can model of organizational choice. *Administrative Science Quarterly, 17*(1).

Cooper, R. G., Edgett, S. J., & Kleinschmidt, E. J. (2001). *Portfolio management for new products* (2nd ed.). Cambridge, MA: Basic Books.

Coulon, M., Ernst, H., Lichtenthaler, U., & Vollmoeller, J. (2009). An overview of tools for managing the corporate innovation portfolio. *International Journal of Technology Intelligence and Planning, 5*(2), 221–239.

Dane, E., & Pratt, M. G. (2007). Exploring intuition and its role in managerial decision making. *Academy of Management Review, 32*(1), 33–54.

Davenport, T. H. (2006). Competing on analytics. *Harvard Business Review, 84*(1), 98–107.

Dean, J. W., & Sharfman, M. P. (1996). Does decision process matter? A study of strategic decision-making effectiveness. *Academy of Management Journal, 39*(2), 368–392.

Debes, J. L. (1969). The loom of visual literacy. *Audiovisual Instruction,* 14(8), 25–27.

Dodgson, M., Gann, D., & Salter, A. J. (2005). *Think, play, do: Technology, innovation, and organization.* New York, NY: Oxford University Press.

Doerner, D. (1989). *Die logik des misslingens: Strategisches denken in komplexen situationen.* Hamburg, Germany: Rowohlt Verlag.

Duncan, R. B. (1972). Characteristics of organizational environments and perceived environmental uncertainty. *Administrative Science Quarterly, 17*(3), 313–327.

Dye, L., & Pennypacker, J. S. (1999). An introduction to project portfolio management. In L. Dye & J. S. Pennypacker (Eds.), *Project portfolio management* (pp. 11–16). West Chester, PA: Center for Business Practices.

Eco, U. (1979). Can television teach? *Screen Education,* 31, 15–24.

Edwards, P. A. (2010). Reconceptualizing literacy. *Reading Today, 27*(6), 22.

Eisenhardt, K. M., & Zbaracki, M. J. (1992). Strategic decision making. *Strategic Management Journal, 13*(S2), 17–37.

Eppler, M. J. (2006). A comparison between concept maps, mind maps, conceptual diagrams, and visual metaphors as complementary tools for knowledge construction and sharing. *Information Visualization, 5*(3), 202–210.

Eppler, M. J., & Burkhard, R. A. (2007). Visual representations in knowledge management: Framework and cases. *Journal of Knowledge Management, 11*(4), 112–122.

Eskerod, P., Blichfeldt, B. S., & Toft, A. S. (2004). *Questioning the rational assumption underlying decision-making within project portfolio management literature.* Paper presented at the PMI® Research Conference, London, England.

Ewenstein, B., & Whyte, J. (2009). Knowledge practices in design: The role of visual representations as 'epistemic objects'. *Organization Studies, 30*(1), 7–30.

Fairphone. (2013). *The cost breakdown of the first fairphone.* Retrieved from http://www.fairphone.com/wp-content/uploads/2014/09/Fairphone_Cost_Breakdown_and_Key_Sept2013.pdf

Few, S. (2006). *Information dashboard design: The effective visual communication of data.* Sebastopol, CA: O'Reilly Media.

Few, S. (2010). Our irresistible fascination with all things circular. *Perceptual Edge Visual Business Intelligence Newsletter,* 1–9.

Fischhoff, B. (2006). Visualizing your vulnerabilities. *Harvard Business Review, 84*(5), 28, 30.

Foreman, E., & Selly, M. A. (2002). *Decision by objectives.* Singapore: World Scientific Publishing Company.

136

Foss, S. K. (2004). Framing the study of visual rhetoric: Toward a transformation of rhetorical theory. In C. A. Hill & M. Helmers (Eds.), *Defining visual rhetorics* (pp. 303–313). Mahwah, NJ: Routledge.

Fredrickson, J. W. (1985). Effects of decision motive and organizational performance level on strategic decision processes. *Academy of Management Journal, 28*(4), 821–843.

Friendly, M., & Denis, D. J. (2001). *Milestones in the history of thematic cartography, statistical graphics, and data visualization.* Retrieved from http://www.datavis.ca/milestones/

Geraldi, J. (2008). *Reconciling order and chaos in multi-project firms: Empirical studies on CoPS producers.* Göttingen, Germany: Sierke Verlag.

Geraldi, J., & Arlt, M. (2013). *Can you see the forest for the trees? Supporting sense-making through the visualization of project portfolios.* Paper presented at the IRNOP, Oslo, Norway.

Geraldi, J., & Lechler, T. (2012). Gantt charts revisited: A critical analysis of its roots and implications to the management of projects today. *International Journal of Managing Projects in Business, 5*(4), 578–594.

Geraldi, J., Lee-Kelley, L., & Kutsch, E. (2010). The *Titanic* sank, so what? Project manager response to unexpected events. *International Journal of Project Management, 28*(6), 547–558.

Geraldi, J., Maylor, H., & Williams, T. (2011). Now, let's make it really complex (complicated): A systematic review of the complexities of projects. *International Journal of Operations & Production Management, 31*(9), 966–990.

Geraldi, J. W. (1991). *Portos de passagem.* São Paulo, Brazil: Martins Fontes.

Gersick, C. (1988). Time and transition in work teams: Toward a new model of group development. *Academy of Management Journal,* 31(1), 9–41.

Goffman, E. (1974). *Frame analysis: An essay on the organization of experience.* Cambridge, MA: Harvard University Press.

Gray, D. (2008). Why PowerPoint rules the business world: Call for visual literacy. Retrieved from http://www.davegrayinfo.com/2008/05/22/why-powerpoint-rules-the-business-world/

Groenveld, P. (1997). Roadmapping integrated business and technology. *Research Technology Management, 40*(5), 48–55.

Grossklags, J. (2007). *Experimental economics and experimental computer science: A survey.* Paper presented at the Workshop on Experimental Computer Science (ExpCS'07), ACM Federated Computer Research Conference (FCRC), San Diego, CA, USA. June 13–14, 2007.

Halford, G. S., Baker, R., McCredden, J. E., & Bain, J. D. (2005). How many variables can humans process? *Psychological Science, 16*(1), 70–76.

Hall, C.C., Ariss, L., & Todorov, A. (2007). The illusion of knowledge: When more information reduces accuracy and increases confidence. *Organizational Behavior and Human Decision Processes,* 103, 277–290.

Harrison, P. D., & Harrell, A. (1993). Impact of "adverse selection" on managers' project evaluation decisions. *Academy of Management Journal, 36*(3), 635–643.

Healey, C. G. (2012). Attention and visual memory in visualization and computer graphics. *IEEE Transactions on Visualization and Computer Graphics, 18*(7), 1170–1188.

Henderson, K. (1999). *On line and on paper: Visual representations, visual culture, and computer graphics in design engineering.* Cambridge, MA: MIT Press.

Hill, C. A. (2004). The psychology of rhetorical images. In C. A. Hill & M. Helmers (Eds.), *Defining visual rhetorics* (pp. 25–40). Mahwah, NJ: Lawrence Erlbaum Associates.

Huff, D. (1954). *How to lie with statistics*: New York, NY: W. W. Norton & Company.

Insabato, A., Pannunzi, M., Rolls, E. T., & Deco, G. (2010). Confidence-related decision making. *Journal of Neurophysiology, 104*(1), 539–547.

International Telecommunication Union. (2013). *Trends in telecommunication reform 2013: Transnational aspects of regulation in a networked society.* Geneva, Switzerland: International Telecommunication Union.

Jarvenpaa, S. L. (1989). The effect of task demands and graphical format on information processing strategies. *Management Science, 35*(3), 285–303.

Jarvenpaa, S. L. (1990). Graphic displays in decision making—The visual salience effect. *Journal of Behavioral Decision Making, 3*(4), 247–262.

Jarvenpaa, S. L., & Dickson, G. W. (1988). Graphics and managerial decision making: Research-based guidelines. *Communications of the ACM, 31*(6), 764–774.

Johnson, B., & Shneiderman, B. (1991). *Treemaps: A space-filling approach to the visualization of hierarchical information structures.* Paper presented at the 2nd International IEEE Visualization Conference, San Diego, CA, USA.

Justesen, L., & Mouritsen, J. (2009). The triple visual: Translations between photographs, 3-D visualizations and calculations. *Accounting, Auditing & Accountability Journal, 22*(6), 973–990.

Kaplan, S. (2011). Strategy and PowerPoint: An inquiry into the epistemic culture and machinery of strategy making. *Organization Science, 22*(2), 320–346.

Keim, D., Kohlhammer, J., Ellis, G., & Mansmann, F. (2010). *Mastering the information age: Solving problems with visual analytics.* Goslar, Germany: Eurographics Association.

Kester, L., Griffin, A., Hultink, E. J., & Lauche, K. (2011). Exploring portfolio decision-making processes. *Journal of Product Innovation Management, 28*(5), 641–661.

Killen, C. (2013). Evaluation of project interdependency visualization through decision scenario experimentation. *International Journal of Project Management, 31*, 804–816.

Kirschner, P. A., Shum, B. S. J., & Carr, C. S. (2003). *Visualizing argumentation: Software tools for collaborative and educational sense-making.* London, England: Springer.

138

Klayman, J., Soll, J. B., González-Vallejo, C., & Barlas, S. (1999). Overconfidence: It depends on how, what, and whom you ask. *Organizational Behavior and Human Decision Processes, 79*(3), 216–247.

Klein, G., Moon, B., & Hoffman, R. R. (2006a). Making sense of sensemaking 1: Alternative perspectives. *Intelligent Systems, IEEE, 21*(4), 70–73.

Klein, G., Moon, B., & Hoffman, R. R. (2006b). Making sense of sensemaking 2: A macrocognitive model. *Intelligent Systems, IEEE, 21*(5), 88–92.

Klein, G., Phillips, J. K., Raill, E. L., & Peluso, D. A. (2007). A data-frame theory of sensemaking. In R. R. Hoffman (Ed.), *Expertise out of context: Proceedings of the sixth international conference on naturalistic decision making* (pp. 113–158). New York, NY: Taylor & Francis.

Kress, G., & Van Leeuwen, T. (1996). *Reading images:* The grammar of visual design. London, England: Routledge.

Larkin, J. H., & Simon, H. A. (1987). Why a diagram is (sometimes) worth ten thousand words. *Cognitive Science, 11*(1), 65–100.

Lau, A., & Moere, A. V. (2007, July). *Towards a model of information aesthetics in information visualization.* Information Visualization 11th International Conference, Zürich, Switzerland.

LaValle, S., Lesser, E., Shockley, R., Hopkins, M. S., & Kruschwitz, N. (2011). Big data, analytics and the path from insights to value. *MIT Sloan Management Review, 52(2),* Retrieved from http://sloanreview.mit.edu/article/big-data-analytics-and-the-path-from-insights-to-value/

Lengler, R., & Eppler, M. J. (2007). A periodic table of visualization methods. Retrieved from http://www.visual-literacy.org/periodic_table/periodic_table.html

Levine, H. A. (2005). *Project portfolio management.* San Francisco, CA: John Wiley & Sons.

Loch, C., DeMeyer, A., & Pich, M. (2006). *Managing the unknown: A new approach to managing high uncertainty and risk in projects.* New York, NY: John Wiley & Sons.

Lurie, N. H., & Mason, C. H. (2007). Visual representation: Implications for decision making. *Journal of Marketing, 71*(1), 160–177.

MacNeice, E. H. (1951). *Production forecasting, planning and control.* New York, NY: John Wiley & Sons, Inc.

Markowitz, H. (1952). Portfolio selection. *The Journal of Finance, 7*(1), 77–91.

Martinsuo, M. (2013). Project portfolio management in practice and in context. *International Journal of Project Management, 31*(6), 794–803.

Martinsuo, M., & Lehtonen, P. (2007). Role of single-project management in achieving portfolio management efficiency. *International Journal of Project Management, 25*(1), 56–65.

Maylor, H., Geraldi, J. G., Johnson, M., & Turner, N. (2009). *Mind the gap: Temporal disconnects in the provision of complex service offerings.* Paper presented at the EUROMA 2008 University of Groningen, Netherlands.

Maylor, H., Turner, N., & Murray-Webster, R. (2013). How hard can it be? Actively managing complexity in technology projects. *Research-Technology Management, 56*(4), 45–51.

Mazza, R. (2009). *Introduction to information visualization*. New York, NY: Springer-Verlag Inc.

McAfee, A., Brynjolfsson, E., Davenport, T. H., Patil, D. J., & Barton, D. (2012). Big data: The management revolution. *Harvard Business Review, 90*(10), 61–67.

McCandless, D. (2009). *Information is beautiful*. New York, NY: Harper Collins.

McCray, G., Purvis, R., & McCray, C. (2002). Project management under uncertainty: The impact of heuristics and biases. *Project Management Journal, 33*(1), 49–57.

McQuarrie, E. F., & Mick, D. G. (1999). Visual rhetoric in advertising: Text-interpretive, experimental, and reader-response analyses. *Journal of Consumer Research, 26*(1), 37–54.

Messaris, P. (1997). *Visual persuasion: The role of images in advertising*. Thousand Oaks, CA: Sage Publications.

Meyer, R. E., Höllerer, M. A., Jancsary, D., & Van Leeuwen, T. (2013). The visual dimension in organizing, organization, and organization research: Core ideas, current developments, and promising avenues. *The Academy of Management Annals, 7*(1), 487–553.

Midalia, S. (1999). Textualising gender. *Interpretations, 32*(1), 27–32.

Mitchell, W. J. T. (1994). *Picture theory: Essays on verbal and visual representation*. Chicago, IL: University of Chicago Press.

Neri, G. (2001). Ethics and photography. *The Digital Journalism* (01). Retrieved from http://digitaljournalist.org/issue0101/neri.htm

Newell, A. (1990). *Unified theories of cognition*. Cambridge, MA: Harvard University Press.

Nicolini, D., Mengis, J., & Swan, J. (2012). Understanding the role of objects in cross-disciplinary collaboration. *Organization Science, 23*(3), 612–629.

Norrie, J. (2006). *Improving results of project portfolio management in the public sector using a balanced strategic scoring model*. (Doctoral dissertation). RMIT University, Melbourne, Australia.

Omodei, M., Elliott, G., Clancy, J. M., Wearing, A. J., & McLennan, J. (2005). More is better? A bias toward overuse of resources in naturalistic decision-making settings. In H. Montgomery, R. Lipshitz & B. Brehmer (Eds.), *How professionals make decisions* (pp. 29–42). Mahwah, NJ: Lawrence Erlbaum Associates.

O'Reilly, C., Bustard, D., & Morrow, P. (2005). *The war room command console: Shared visualizations for inclusive team coordination*. Paper presented at the Proceedings of the 2005 ACM symposium on Software visualization, St. Louis, MO, USA.

Parasuraman, A., Berry, L. L., & Zeithaml, V. A. (1991). Refinement and reassessment of the SERVQUAL scale. *Journal of Retailing, 67*(4), 420–450.

Parasuraman, A., Zeithaml, V. A., & Berry, L. L. (1988). Servqual: A multiple-item scale for measuring consumer perceptions of service quality. *Journal of Retailing, 64*(1), 12–40.

Pauwels, L. (2006). A theoretical framework for assessing visual representational practices in knowledge building and science communications.

140

In L. Pauwels (Ed.), *Visual cultures of science: Rethinking representational practices in knowledge building and science communication* (pp. 1–25). Hanover, NH: Dartmouth College Press.

Perrow, C. (1999). *Normal accidents: Living with high-risk technologies.* Princeton, NJ: Princeton University Press.

Petit, Y., & Hobbs, B. (2010). Project portfolios in dynamic environments: Sources of uncertainty and sensing mechanisms. *Project Management Journal, 41*(4), 46–58.

Phillips, B. J., & McQuarrie, E. F. (2004). Beyond visual metaphor: A new typology of visual rhetoric in advertising. *Marketing Theory, 4*(1–2), 113–136.

Playfair, W. (1786). *The commercial and political atlas: Representing, by means of stained copper-plate charts, the progress of the commerce, revenues, expenditure and debts of England during the whole of the eighteenth century.* London, England.

Potters, J., & Van Winden, F. (2000). Professionals and students in a lobbying experiment: Professional rules of conduct and subject surrogacy. *Journal of Economic Behavior & Organization, 43*(4), 499–522.

Powell, T. C., Lovallo., D, & Fox, C. R. (2011). Behavioral strategy. *Strategic Management Journal, 32*(13), 1369–1386.

Project Management Institute. (2013). *PMI's industry growth forecast.* Retrieved from http://www.pmi.org/~/media/PDF/Business-Solutions/PMI_Industry_Growth_Forecase_2010-2010.ashx

Puyou, F. R., Quattrone, P., McLean, C., & Thrift, N. (2012). *Imagining organizations: Performative imagery in business and beyond.* New York, NY: Routledge.

Raab, J. (2008). *Visuelle Wissenssoziologie: Theoretische konzeption und material analysen.* Konstanz, Germany: UVK.

Rams, D. (2013). *Dieter Rams: Ten principles for good design.* Retrieved from https://www.vitsoe.com/eu/about/good-design

Rudolph, J. W. (2003). *Into the big muddy and out again.* (Doctoral dissertation), Boston College, Boston, MA.

Sadler-Smith, E., & Shefy, E. (2004). The intuitive executive: Understanding and applying 'gut feel' in decision making. *Academy of Management Executive, 18*(4), 76–91.

Schmidt, R. L. (1993). A model for R&D project selection with combined benefit, outcome, and resource interactions. *IEEE Transactions on Engineering Management, 40*(1), 403–410.

Schranger, J. E., & Madansky, A. (2013). Behavioral strategy: A foundational view. *Journal of Strategy and Management, 6*(1), 81–95.

Shneiderman, B. (1996, September). *The eyes have it: A task by data type taxonomy for information visualizations.* In IEEE Proceedings of Symposium on Visual Languages, pp. 336–343, September 3–6, 1996, Boulder, CO.

Shook, J. (2009). Toyota's secret: The A3 report. *MIT Sloan Management Review, 50*(4), 30–33.

Shore, B. (2008). Systematic biases and culture in project failures. *Project Management Journal, 39*(4), 5–16.

Simkin, D., & Hastie, R. (1987). An information-processing analysis of graph perception. *Journal of the American Statistical Association, 82*(398), 454–465.

Simon, H. A. (1955). A behavioral model of rational choice. *Quarterly Journal of Economics, 69*, 99–118.

Smelcer, J. B., & Carmel, E. (1997). The effectiveness of different representations for managerial problem solving: Comparing tables and maps. *Decision Sciences,28*(2), 391–420.

Spence, I. (2005). No humble pie: The origins and usage of a statistical chart. *Journal of Education and Behavioral Statistics, 30*(4), 353–368.

Spence, I., & Lewandowsky, S. (1991). Displaying proportions and percentages. *Applied Cognitive Psychology, 5*, 61–77.

Spiegelhalter, D., Pearson, M., & Short, I. (2011). Visualizing uncertainty about the future. Science, *333*(6048), 1393–1400.

Snow, J. (1854). *On the mode of communication of cholera* (2nd ed.). London, England: C. F. Cheffins. Retrieved from http://matrix.msu.edu/~johnsnow/images/online_companion/chapter_images/fig12-5.jpg

Snowden, D., & Boone, M. E. (2007). A leader's framework for decision making. *Harvard Business Review, 85*(11), 68–76.

Stacey, R. O. (1995). The science of complexity: An alternative perspective for strategic change processes. *Strategic Management Journal,* 16(6), 477–495.

Staw, B. M. (1981). The escalation of commitment to a course of action. *Academy of Management Review, 6*(4), 577–587.

Steele, J., M. (2005). Darrell Huff and fifty years of how to lie with statistics. *Statistical Science, 20*(3), 205–209.

Steele, J., & Iliinsky, N. (2010). *Beautiful visualization: Looking at data through the eyes of experts*. Sebastopol, CA: O'Reilly.

Taxén, L., & Lilliesköld, J. (2008). Images as action instruments in complex projects. *International Journal of Project Management, 26*(5), 527–536.

Tsai, C. I., Klayman, J., & Hastie, R. (2008). Effects of amount of information on judgment accuracy and confidence. *Organizational Behavior and Human Decision Processes, 107*(2), 97–105.

Tufte, E. R. (2001). *The visual display of quantitative information* (2nd ed.). Cheshire, CT: Graphics Press.

Tversky, A., & Kahneman, D. (1974). Judgment under uncertainty: Heuristics and biases. *Science, 185*(4157), 1124.

Verma, D., & Sinha, K. K. (2002). Toward a theory of project interdependencies in high tech R&D environments. *Journal of Operations Management, 20*(5), 451–468.

Ward, J., & Daniel, E. (2005). Benefits management: Delivering value from IS & IT investments. Chichester, England: Wiley.

Ward, M., Grinstein, G., & Keim, D. (2010). *Interactive data visualization: Foundations, techniques, and applications*. Boca Raton, FL: Taylor & Francis.

Ware, C. (2012). *Information visualisation: Perception for design* (3rd ed.). Amsterdam, Netherlands: Morgan Kaufmann.

Wattenberg, M., & Viegas, F. B. (2008). Emerging graphic tool gets people talking. *Harvard Business Review, 86*(5), 30–32.

142 Weick, K. E. (1995). *Sensemaking in organizations*. Thousand Oaks, CA: Sage Publications.

Weick, K. E., & Sutcliffe, K. M. (2001). *Managing the unexpected: Assuring high performance in an age of complexity*. San Francisco, CA: Jossey-Bass.

Weick, K. E., Sutcliffe, K. M., & Obstfeld, D. (2005). Organizing and the process of sensemaking. *Organization Science, 16*(4), 409.

Whitehouse, D. (2000). Ice Age star map discovered. *BBC News*. Retrieved from http://news.bbc.co.uk/2/hi/science/nature/871930.stm

Whyte, J., Ewenstein, B., Hales, M., & Tidd, J. (2008). Visualizing knowledge in project-based work. *Long Range Planning, 41*(1), 74–92.

Yakura, E. K. (2002). Charting time: Timelines as temporal boundary objects. *Academy of Management Journal, 45*(5), 956–970.

Yakura, E. K. (2013). Visualizing an information technology project: The role of PowerPoint presentations over time. *Information and Organization, 23*(4), 258–276.

Yau, N. (2011). *Visualize this: The FlowingData guide to design, visualization, and statistics*. Indianapolis, IN: Wiley.

Yigitbasioglu, O. M., & Velcu, O. (2012). A review of dashboards in performance management: Implications for design and research. *International Journal of Accounting Information Systems, 13*(1), 41–59.

Zhou, M. X., & Feiner, S. K. (1998). *Visual task characterization for automated visual discourse synthesis*. CHI '98 Proceedings of the SIGCHI Conference on Human Factors in Computing Systems, pp. 392–399, April 18-23, 1998, Los Angeles, CA, USA.

Authors

Joana Geraldi

Dr. Joana Geraldi is Associate Professor at Engineering Systems Group, DTU Management Engineering, Denmark, and Honorary Senior Research Associate at the Bartlett School of Construction and Project Management at University College London (UCL).

Joana previously held positions as lecturer at UCL, research fellow at Cranfield School of Management, and research assistant at University of Siegen, Germany. She studied engineering management at UFSCar, Brazil, and earned her doctoral degree from the University of Siegen. Her dissertation has earned research awards from the Association for Project Management (APM) and the International Project Management Association (IPMA).

Joana has over 10 years of experience in project management research. Her current research interest lies in creating a fruitful context for projects, including portfolio and program management, the impact of visuals in organizations, complexity, and flexibility.

Joana has worked closely with companies such as MAN Ferrostaal, ThyssenKrupp Uhde, Voith, and Hewlett-Packard, and believes that there is room for a more fruitful conversation between theory and practice, and the development of rigorous research with relevance to practice.

Mario Arlt

Dr. Mario Arlt, DPM, MS, PMP, is a Global Practice Leader, Operational Excellence for ABB, and Honorary Lecturer at the Bartlett School of Construction and Project Management at University College London (UCL).

Mario previously held positions at ESI International, SIEMENS, PWC, and KPMG. He holds a doctorate in project management from RMIT University, Melbourne, Australia, and a master's degree in economics from Universitaet Konstanz, Germany.

For over 15 years, Mario has been a practitioner, consultant, trainer, and coach in the areas of project, program, and portfolio management. Mario has supported the *Project Management Institute* as a contributor in the development of the *Standard for Project Portfolio Management* and the roll-out of *OPM3* ProductSuite®.

Mario's research focuses on portfolio management, project management maturity models, and procurement management. In his doctoral thesis, Mario applied experimental research methods to project portfolio management, a first in project management research.